Complete Chicken Cookbook

Complete Chicken Cookbook

Holly Farms®

The Benjamin Company, Inc.

Front cover photo: Crispy Nuggets (page 19),
Barbecued Drummettes (page 20).
Back cover photo: Southern Fried Chicken (page 38).

Editor-in-Chief:	Barbara Bloch
Recipe Development:	Rita Barrett
Managing Editor:	Virginia Schomp
Editorial Assistant:	Carol Grumbach
Production Manager:	Pat Drew
Photography:	Gordon E. Smith
Cooking for Photography:	Marina Freyer
Styling for Photography:	Elaine Smith
Art & Design:	Tom Brecklin
Illustrations.	Barb Schwoegler
Typography:	A-Line, Milwaukee

Produced and Published by The Benjamin Company, Inc.
One Westchester Plaza
Elmsford, New York 10523

ISBN: 0-87502-130-1
Library of Congress Catalog Card Number: 84-070799

Printed in the United States of America
First Printing: August, 1984

Holly-Pak® is a trademark of Holly Farms Poultry Industries, Inc., Wilkesboro,
North Carolina.

CONTENTS

Dear Reader:

"I found the COMPLETE CHICKEN COOKBOOK fun and instructive, as well as quite useful. As chicken fanciers after my own heart, the folks at Holly Farms believe in one of my favorite maxims 'Waste Not Want Not,' in considering the many ways chicken can be used. They even show you how to save wings, tips and extra parts to make your own stock. And they give you hints on how to save time by telling you not only which steps of the delectable dishes can be prepared ahead of time, but how to prepare the same dish in the microwave, if you so choose — instead of in the the oven or on top of the stove.

"This new cookbook is varied and imaginative and full of new ideas (and we all need those). Some of my favorites are Devilish Drumsticks, Boneless Thighs Cordon Bleu, and of course, Southern Fried Chicken. I expect if you drop in my house (unexpected or otherwise), you will find how I put these delicious ideas from Holly Farms to use."

Warmest Regards,

Dinah Shore

Chafing Dish Franks, Petite Chicken and Almond Cut-Outs (page 10), Chicken and Cheese Stuffed Mushrooms (page 11).

Appetizers

CHAFING DISH FRANKS

48 appetizers

1 package (16 ounces)
   Holly Farms Chicken
   Franks
1 jar (10 ounces) red
   currant or plum jelly

1 jar (5 ounces) mild or
   spicy brown mustard
2 tablespoons bourbon
   (optional)

Cut each chicken frank into 6 pieces and set aside. Place jelly and mustard in medium-size saucepan and cook over low heat, stirring constantly, until jelly is melted and mixture is well blended. Stir in bourbon, add chicken franks, stir well, and simmer 5 minutes, being careful not to allow sauce to burn. Spoon into chafing dish and serve hot with cocktail picks.

Microwave Method: Prepare chicken franks as directed above. Place jelly and mustard in 1 1/2-quart microproof casserole. Cover loosely and microcook at 100% power 6 minutes, stirring after 3 minutes. Stir in bourbon, add chicken franks, stir well, recover, and microcook at 100% power 2 minutes. Spoon into chafing dish and serve as directed above.

PETITE CHICKEN-ALMOND CUT-OUTS

40 appetizers

1 cup ground cooked
   chicken (page 93)
1/4 cup minced celery
1/4 cup ground almonds
1/4 cup mayonnaise
1 teaspoon lemon juice
   salt and white pepper
   to taste

20 slices very thin white
   or whole-wheat bread
   softened whipped butter
   pimiento strips
   sliced olives
   tiny dill sprigs

Combine chicken, celery, almonds, mayonnaise, lemon juice, salt, and pepper. Mix well and set aside. Trim crusts from bread. Spread butter lightly on 10 slices of bread. Spread chicken mixture evenly over remaining 10 slices and sandwich together. Cut each "sandwich" into decorative shapes with sharp 1 1/2-inch decorative cookie or canapé cutter. Garnish each cut-out with pimiento strip, sliced or chopped olive, or dill sprig. Serve cold.

Variation: Use 10 slices white bread and 10 slices whole-wheat bread. Spread chicken mixture on white bread and top each "sandwich" with buttered whole-wheat bread.

CHICKEN AND CHEESE STUFFED MUSHROOMS

40 appetizers

40 medium-size mushrooms
(1 1/2 to 2 inches in
diameter)
5 tablespoons butter or
margarine, divided
1 small onion, minced
1/4 cup finely chopped
celery
2 teaspoons lemon juice
1 cup ground cooked
chicken (page 93)
3 tablespoons mayonnaise
2 tablespoons plain yogurt
or dairy sour cream

1 tablespoon freshly
minced parsley
1 tablespoon snipped
chives
hot pepper sauce to
taste
salt and freshly ground
pepper to taste
3/4 cup grated Swiss or
Gruyère cheese, divided
paprika

Wipe mushrooms with damp cloth and trim ends. Remove stems, set mushroom caps aside, and finely chop stems. Melt 2 tablespoons butter in skillet, add chopped mushroom stems, onion, and celery, and sauté until onion is transparent. Remove from heat and sprinkle with lemon juice. Preheat oven to 375°F. Place mushroom-onion mixture, chicken, mayonnaise, yogurt, parsley, chives, hot pepper sauce, salt, and pepper in bowl, and mix well. Add 1/2 cup cheese and stir until well mixed. Melt remaining 3 tablespoons butter and use to brush reserved mushroom caps. Fill mushrooms with chicken mixture, mounding stuffing in center, and arrange in large, shallow baking dish, stuffing side up. Sprinkle top of each mushroom with remaining 1/4 cup grated cheese. Bake 12 to 15 minutes or until mushrooms are just tender and cheese is melted. Let cool 2 to 3 minutes. Sprinkle with paprika and arrange on serving dish. Serve hot.

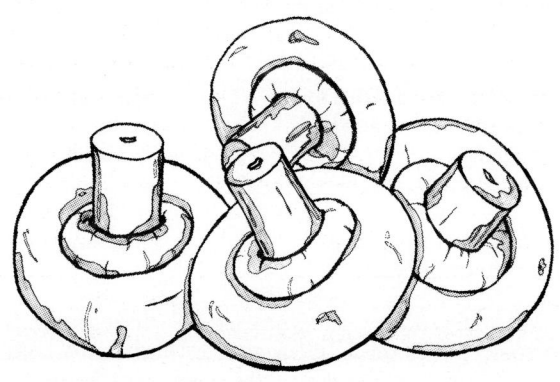

CHICKEN FILLED PASTRY SQUARES
32 appetizers

2 tablespoons butter or margarine	1 tablespoon freshly chopped parsley
1/2 cup chopped mushrooms	1/2 teaspoon ground ginger
1/4 cup thinly sliced scallions	2/3 cup homemade chicken stock (page 24) or canned chicken broth
1 clove garlic, minced	
1 cup finely diced cooked chicken (page 93)	2 tablespoons soy sauce
1/4 cup chopped bamboo shoots	1 tablespoon dry sherry
	2 tablespoons cornstarch
2 tablespoons minced water chestnuts	1 package (17 1/4 ounces) frozen puff pastry, thawed

Melt butter in skillet, add mushrooms, scallions, and garlic, and sauté 3 to 4 minutes. Add chicken, bamboo shoots, water chestnuts, parsley, and ginger, and stir well. Place chicken stock, soy sauce, sherry, and cornstarch in small bowl, and mix until smooth. Add to skillet and cook over low heat, stirring, until thickened. Remove skillet from heat and set aside to cool. Preheat oven to 400°F. Unfold 1 sheet of pastry and lay flat on lightly floured surface. Roll out pastry with lightly floured rolling pin to 12-inch square. Cut pastry into sixteen 3-inch squares. Spoon 1 teaspoon chicken filling onto center of each square. Lightly brush edges of each square with water. Fold pastry over filling to make rectangles and press edges together with fork to seal. Repeat with remaining pastry and filling. Place filled pastries on ungreased cookie sheets. Bake 16 to 18 minutes or until golden brown. Remove pastries to wire racks and let cool 10 minutes before serving.

CHICKEN YAKITORI
24 to 26 appetizers

4 Holly Farms Boneless Chicken Breasts or 6 to 8 Boneless Chicken Thigh Fillets	3 tablespoons sweet white wine (sauterne or mirin)
3 tablespoons vegetable oil	1 container Holly Farms Chicken Livers, toasted sesame seed to serve (optional)
5 tablespoons soy sauce	
5 tablespoons sugar	

Place 24 to 26 wooden skewers, each 5 inches long, in bowl of water to soak. Set aside. Cut breasts or thighs into 1-inch cubes. Heat oil in skillet, add chicken cubes, and sauté over high heat 3 minutes, stirring occasionally. Combine soy sauce, sugar, and wine. Add to skillet and cook 4 minutes, stirring occasionally to coat chicken. Remove chicken with slotted spoon and set aside. Preheat oven to 400°F. Rinse chicken livers under cold running water. Pat dry with paper towels and cut each liver in half. Add to skillet and cook, stirring, until livers are no longer pink. Remove livers with slotted spoon and set aside. Reserve liquid in skillet. Remove skewers from water and thread alternate pieces of chicken and liver onto skewers, beginning and ending with chicken. Arrange skewers in single layer in roasting pan, brush with reserved cooking liquid, and bake 8 to 10 minutes or until heated through. Serve with shallow dish of toasted sesame seed. Roll filled skewers in sesame seed before eating.

CHICKEN TOTS
about 24 appetizers

4 cups ground cooked
    chicken (page 93)
1/2 cup cooked rice
1/4 cup plain dry bread
    crumbs
1 small onion, grated
2 tablespoons freshly
    minced parsley

1/2 teaspoon ground cumin
1/2 teaspoon paprika
1/4 teaspoon turmeric
    salt and white pepper
    to taste
2 eggs, beaten
4 to 6 tablespoons vegetable
    oil

Combine chicken, rice, bread crumbs, onion, parsley, cumin, paprika, turmeric, salt, and pepper, and stir until well mixed. Add eggs and stir until mixture is well blended and binds together. Shape chicken mixture into walnut-size balls. Heat oil in skillet, add chicken balls, and fry until golden brown on all sides. Remove chicken balls with slotted spoon and drain on paper towels. Arrange on serving dish and serve with cocktail picks.

Tip: These appetizers can be made ahead of time, refrigerated, and reheated in preheated 350°F oven 10 to 12 minutes just before serving.

MINIATURE CHICKEN AND
SHRIMP QUICHES

12 appetizers

Pastry:

2 1/4 cups all-purpose flour
1 teaspoon salt
2/3 cup chilled shortening

5 to 6 tablespoons ice
    water

Filling:

2 tablespoons butter or
    margarine
1 bunch scallions, thinly
    sliced (green tops
    included)
3/4 cup finely diced cooked
    chicken (page 93)
1/4 cup diced cooked shrimp
1 teaspoon tarragon

2 eggs
3/4 cup heavy cream
    salt and freshly ground
    pepper to taste
1 cup shredded Gruyère,
    Jarlsberg, or Swiss
    cheese
12 small shrimp, cooked and
    peeled for garnish

Stir flour and salt in bowl. Cut in shortening with pastry blender or 2 knives until mixture resembles coarse crumbs. Sprinkle with ice water, 1 tablespoon at a time, tossing flour mixture with fork until pastry begins to bind together. Gather dough into ball and divide into 2 equal-size pieces. Wrap each piece in plastic wrap or waxed paper and refrigerate 30 minutes. Roll out each piece of chilled pastry on lightly floured surface to 12-inch circle. Cut each circle into 6 rounds with floured 4-inch fluted cookie cutter. Line 12-cup muffin pan with pastry circles, pressing pastry onto bottom and up sides of muffin cups. Set aside. Preheat oven to 375°F. Melt butter in skillet, add scallions, and sauté 2 to 3 minutes. Combine scallions, chicken, shrimp, and tarragon and mix well. Set aside. Beat eggs, cream, salt, and pepper until just blended. Divide chicken mixture evenly in pastry lined muffin cups. Pour beaten egg mixture evenly over chicken and sprinkle with cheese. Bake 25 to 30 minutes or until well puffed and golden brown. Cool in pan 2 minutes. Carefully run tip of sharp knife around inside edge of each muffin cup and remove quiches from pan. Cool on wire racks 10 minutes. Cut each shrimp in half lengthwise and use to garnish quiche. Serve warm.

Miniature Chicken and Shrimp Quiches,
Chicken Wings with Sweet and Sour Sauce (page 16)

CHICKEN WINGS WITH SWEET AND SOUR SAUCE

28 appetizers

14 Holly Farms Prime Chicken Wings or 28 Prime Chicken Drummettes
2/3 cup all-purpose flour
1 teaspoon garlic powder
1/2 teaspoon dry mustard
salt and freshly ground pepper to taste
1 egg beaten with 1 tablespoon water
vegetable oil for deep-fat frying
1 jar (10 ounces) sweet and sour sauce
1 to 2 tablespoons toasted sesame seed (optional)

Cut off wing tips at first joint and save to make stock or soup. Cut each chicken wing through joint to make 2 pieces. Place flour, garlic powder, mustard, salt, and pepper in plastic bag. Dip 1 chicken piece in beaten egg, shake off excess, place in plastic bag, and shake to coat well. Place on waxed paper. Repeat with remaining chicken pieces. Heat oil in deep-fat fryer and fry chicken pieces, a few at a time, until golden brown on both sides. Remove with slotted spoon, drain on paper towels and place in deep bowl. Place sweet and sour sauce in saucepan over low heat and cook, stirring, just until sauce is heated through. Pour sauce over chicken and toss until coated. Remove chicken to serving platter. Sprinkle chicken with sesame seed.

NOTE: Sweet and sour sauce is available in most supermarkets and oriental food stores.

HOISIN DRUMMETTES

22 appetizers

1 cup dry white wine or dry sherry
1/2 cup soy sauce
1 tablespoon minced garlic
1 teaspoon dry mustard
1 teaspoon ground ginger
22 Holly Farms Prime Chicken Drummettes
1/2 cup Hoisin sauce*
1/2 cup ketchup
1/4 cup firmly packed dark brown sugar

Combine wine, soy sauce, garlic, mustard, and ginger in bowl and blend well. Arrange drummettes in single layer in large, shallow, glass baking dish. Pour marinade over drummettes and turn to coat. Cover and refrigerate several hours or overnight, turning chicken occasionally. Preheat oven to 350°F. Drain off marinade, reserving 1/2 cup. Combine reserved marinade with Hoisin sauce, ketchup, and brown sugar, and mix well. Pour Hoisin mixture over drummettes and turn to coat. Bake 30 to 35 minutes or until tender, basting and turning chicken at least twice during cooking. Arrange drummettes on serving platter and pour sauce in small bowl. Serve as dipping sauce. (Be sure to have a good supply of cocktail napkins available.)

Microwave Method: Prepare marinade as directed above. Arrange drummettes in single layers in two 10-inch round micro-proof dishes, placing thickest portion of drummettes at outer edges of dishes. Pour marinade over drummettes and turn to coat. Cover and refrigerate several hours or overnight, turning chicken occasionally. Drain marinade from both dishes, reserving 1/3 cup. Combine reserved marinade with Hoisin sauce, ketchup, and brown sugar, and mix well. Pour Hoisin mixture over each dish of drummettes and turn to coat. Cover 1 dish loosely, and microcook at 100% power 6 minutes. Turn drummettes over, recover, and microcook at 100% power 6 minutes. Let stand 5 minutes. Repeat with second dish of drummettes. Serve as directed above.

NOTE: Hoisin sauce is available in the Chinese food section of most supermarkets and oriental food stores.

SHANGHAI CHICKEN WINGS   *16 appetizers*

8 **Holly Farms Prime Chicken Wings or 16 Prime Chicken Drummettes**	2 **tablespoons ketchup**
	2 **tablespoons dry sherry**
	1 **teaspoon ground ginger**
	1 **large clove garlic, minced**
1/3 **cup soy sauce**	
2 **tablespoons dark corn syrup**	

Cut off wing tips and save to make stock or soup. Cut each chicken wing through joint to make 2 pieces. Combine soy sauce, corn syrup, ketchup, sherry, ginger, and garlic, and mix until well blended. Arrange chicken wings in single layer in shallow glass baking dish. Pour soy sauce mixture over and turn to coat. Cover and refrigerate several hours or overnight, turning occasionally. Preheat oven to 375°F. Remove chicken wings from refrigerator and uncover. Bake in marinade 25 to 30 minutes or until tender, basting with marinade several times. Remove wings to serving dish and pour marinade into serving bowl. Serve marinade as dipping sauce.

Microwave Method: Prepare and marinate chicken wings as directed above. Arrange wings in 10-inch round, shallow, microproof dish, placing thickest part of wings at outer edge of dish. Cover loosely with plastic wrap and microcook at 100% power 10 minutes, turning wings over after 5 minutes. Let stand 5 minutes on heatproof surface. Serve as directed above.

CRISPY NUGGETS

about 48 appetizers

6 Holly Farms Boneless
  Chicken Breasts
  coating mixture #1 or
  #2 (see below)
  all-purpose flour for
  dredging

1 egg beaten with 1
  tablespoon water
  vegetable oil for
  deep-frying

Cover wire rack with waxed paper and set aside. Cut each breast into 1-inch pieces. Combine ingredients for coating mixture on flat plate and mix well. Dredge chicken pieces in flour, shake off excess, dip in beaten egg, and roll in coating mixture. Place coated chicken pieces on rack and refrigerate 30 minutes or until ready to cook. Heat 2 inches oil in skillet. Add chicken pieces, a few at a time, and deep-fry 2 to 3 minutes. Turn and fry 2 minutes or until golden brown. Remove with slotted spoon and drain on paper towels. Repeat with remaining chicken. Arrange on serving dish and serve with sweet and sour sauce, honey, barbecue sauce, or your favorite dipping sauce.

Coating Mixture #1

1/2 cup all-purpose flour
1/4 cup yellow corn meal
  2 teaspoons garlic powder
    or onion powder
  1 teaspoon paprika

1 teaspoon salt
1/2 teaspoon thyme
1/2 teaspoon oregano
1/4 teaspoon pepper

Combine all ingredients in bowl and mix well.

Coating Mixture #2

1/2 cup cracker meal, matzo
    meal, or plain dry
    bread crumbs
1/4 cup freshly grated
    Parmesan cheese

2 teaspoons Italian
    seasoning
1 teaspoon salt
1 1/2 teaspoons paprika
1/2 teaspoon dry mustard

Combine all ingredients in bowl and mix well.

Crispy Nuggets, Barbecued Drummettes (page 20)

BARBECUED DRUMMETTES

22 appetizers

1 cup hickory-flavored
   barbecue sauce
2 tablespoons prepared
   taco sauce (hot
   preferred)

1 tablespoon brown sugar
1 teaspoon chili powder
22 Holly Farms Prime
   Chicken Drummettes

Combine barbecue sauce, taco sauce, brown sugar, and chili powder in small bowl, and mix until well blended. Set aside. Place chicken on rack in broiler pan and broil 12 minutes, turning once. Brush chicken liberally with sauce and broil 4 to 6 minutes or until tender, turning and brushing with sauce several times during cooking. Let cool about 10 minutes before serving.

Variation: Substitute chicken wings for drummettes. Remove wing tips and reserve for use another time.

NOTE: Chicken can also be cooked on outdoor grill. Place chicken over medium-hot coals and grill 20 to 25 minutes, turning frequently. Brush with sauce during last 10 minutes of cooking only.

CHICKEN LIVER PATE

about 2 cups

1 container Holly Farms
   Chicken Livers
   (approximately 14
   ounces)
4 tablespoons butter or
   rendered chicken fat
   (page 98)
2 cloves garlic, minced
1 cup finely chopped
   onions

salt and freshly ground
   pepper to taste
hot pepper sauce to
   taste
2 hard-cooked eggs,
   coarsely chopped
2 tablespoons sweet sherry
   (optional)
assorted cocktail breads
   and crackers to serve

Lightly grease 2 to 2 1/2-cup mold with vegetable oil or melted chicken fat. Invert mold onto paper towel to drain. Rinse chicken livers under cold running water and pat dry with paper towels. Cut livers in half, trim, and set aside. Melt butter in skillet, add garlic and onions, and sauté 4 minutes. Add chicken livers to skillet and sauté 5 to 7 minutes or until livers are no longer pink. Remove from heat and spoon contents of skillet into container of food processor or blender. Add salt, pepper, and hot pepper sauce, and process 1 minute. Add eggs and sherry, and process until almost smooth. Spoon mixture into prepared mold and smooth top. Cover and refrigerate several hours or until firm. To serve, unmold onto serving dish and surround with cocktail breads and crackers.

Microwave Method: Prepare mold and chicken livers as directed above. Place butter in 1-quart microproof casserole, cover tightly, and microcook at 100% power 1 minute or until melted. Add chicken livers, garlic, and onions, and stir well. Recover and microcook at 100% power 7 minutes or until chicken livers are no longer pink, stirring every 2 1/2 minutes. Spoon contents of casserole into container of food processor or blender and proceed as directed above.

RUMAKI   *24 to 28 appetizers*

1 **container Holly Farms Chicken Livers (approximately 14 ounces)**	**boiling water**
1/4 **cup dry sherry**	2 **cans (6 1/2 ounces each) water chestnuts, drained**
1/4 **cup soy sauce**	12 **to 14 slices bacon, cut in half**
1/2 **teaspoon dry mustard**	**parsley sprigs for garnish (optional)**
1/2 **teaspoon ground ginger hot pepper sauce to taste**	

Rinse chicken livers under cold running water. Pat dry with paper towels and cut each liver in half. Combine sherry, soy sauce, mustard, ginger, and hot pepper sauce. Place chicken livers in glass bowl, pour marinade over, cover, and refrigerate 2 to 3 hours. Remove livers from marinade, discarding marinade. Wrap 1/2 chicken liver and 1 water chestnut in 1/2 slice bacon and secure with wooden toothpick. Arrange wrapped chicken livers on rack in broiler pan. Broil 10 to 12 minutes or until bacon is crisp, turning once. Place on warm serving dish, garnish with parsley sprigs, and serve hot.

Microwave Method: Arrange rumaki in 9-inch round microproof dish and cover with paper towel. Microcook at 100% power 5 minutes. Drain off liquid and rotate dish. Recover and microcook at 100% power 5 minutes. Place rumaki on paper towels to drain. Serve as directed above.

Variations: Substitute pitted dates, softened prunes, or figs for water chestnuts.

HOT CHICKS IN A BLANKET
24 appetizers

1 package (16 ounces)
   Holly Farms Cheese
   Chicken Franks
1 package (8 ounces)
   refrigerator crescent
   rolls

3 to 4 tablespoons
   prepared taco sauce
   (hot or mild)

Cut each chicken frank into 3 pieces and set aside. Separate crescent rolls into 8 triangles and cut each into 3 small triangles. Lightly roll out each small triangle. Preheat oven to 375°F. Cut a small lengthwise slit in center of each piece of chicken frank. Spoon a little taco sauce into each slit. Place 1 piece of chicken frank, filled side down, on corner of crescent triangle and wrap dough around frank. Repeat with remaining dough and chicken franks. Place wrapped chicken franks on ungreased cookie sheet. Bake 16 to 18 minutes or until lightly browned. Remove to wire rack and let cool slightly before serving.

PISTACHIO-CHICKEN DIP
about 2 cups

2 tablespoons butter or
   margarine
1/4 pound mushrooms, chopped
   (1 cup chopped)
1/4 cup thinly sliced
   scallions
4 teaspoons lemon juice
1 cup finely diced cooked
   chicken (page 93)
1/2 cup dairy sour cream or
   plain yogurt

1/2 cup mayonnaise
2 teaspoons curry powder
1/2 teaspoon ground cumin
   salt and freshly ground
   pepper to taste
1/2 cup finely chopped
   pistachio nuts,
   divided

Melt butter in skillet, add mushrooms and scallions, and sauté 3 to 4 minutes. Remove from heat and sprinkle with lemon juice. Place chicken, mushroom-scallion mixture, sour cream, mayonnaise, curry powder, cumin, salt, and pepper in container of blender or food processor, and process to smooth purée. Pour chicken purée into bowl and stir in 1/4 cup chopped nuts. Cover and refrigerate several hours. To serve, spoon dip into serving bowl, sprinkle with remaining 1/4 cup chopped nuts, and surround with assorted crackers, chips, cocktail bread, or raw vegetables.

Basic Chicken Stock (page 24)

Soups and Stocks

BASIC CHICKEN STOCK   *about 12 cups*

1 Holly Farms Hen, Roaster, or Whole Fryer
2 tablespoons salt
1 large onion, studded with 6 whole cloves
2 stalks celery, cut into large chunks (leaves included)
1 large carrot, cut into chunks
6 sprigs parsley (stems included)
10 peppercorns
2 cloves garlic
1 bay leaf

Remove giblets and neck from chicken and rinse under cold running water. Place chicken, giblets, and neck in stockpot or large Dutch oven. Pour in 4 quarts cold water, cover, and bring to a boil. Skim surface of soup. Reduce heat, add salt, onion, celery, carrot, parsley, peppercorns, garlic, and bay leaf. Simmer, uncovered, 3 hours, skimming surface several times during cooking. (Add more water as necessary.) Remove chicken and set aside to cool. Line fine mesh strainer with double thickness of cheesecloth and strain stock into large bowl. Discard vegetables. Measure stock and pour into several rigid containers, allowing space on top for expansion. Cover containers, label, indicating number of cups in each container, and date. Set aside to cool. When cool, place in freezer up to 4 to 6 months or in refrigerator about 4 days. When chicken is cool enough to handle, remove and discard skin and bones. Divide meat if desired, wrap, label, and store in refrigerator up to 2 days or in freezer, in an airtight container, for up to 4 months. Use in salad, soup, casseroles, or any recipe that calls for cooked, cubed, shredded, or ground chicken.

CHICKEN AND BARLEY SOUP   *6 servings*

7 cups homemade chicken stock (above) or canned chicken broth
1/2 cup pearl barley, rinsed salt and freshly ground pepper to taste
1 large onion, chopped
3 carrots, thinly sliced
3 stalks celery, chopped
1 white turnip, coarsely chopped
2 1/2 to 3 cups shredded or cubed cooked chicken (page 93)
1/4 cup freshly chopped parsley

Place stock in large saucepan and bring to a boil. Reduce heat, add barley, salt, and pepper, and simmer 1 hour. Skim surface of soup if necessary. Add onion, carrots, celery, turnip, chicken, and parsley. Simmer 30 minutes or until vegetables are tender. Adjust seasoning and ladle into soup bowls. Serve with crusty French bread.

CREAM OF CHICKEN SOUP   *4 to 6 servings*

4 tablespoons butter or
   margarine
1/4 cup all-purpose flour
1 1/2 cups light cream or half
   and half
4 cups homemade chicken
   stock (page 24) or
   canned chicken broth
1/4 teaspoon nutmeg
   salt and freshly ground
   pepper to taste

1 cup shredded or finely
   diced cooked chicken
   (page 93)
1/3 cup dry sherry
1 to 2 tablespoons freshly
   chopped parsley or
   tarragon for garnish
   seasoned croutons for
   garnish

Melt butter in large saucepan. Add flour and cook over moderate heat 1 minute, stirring. Add cream slowly, stirring constantly. Slowly add stock. Season with nutmeg, salt, and pepper. Cook over low heat, stirring, until slightly thickened. Add chicken and sherry and simmer 5 minutes. Ladle into soup bowls, sprinkle with parsley, and garnish with croutons.

CHICKEN LIVER AND
GIBLET SOUP   *6 to 8 servings*

1 package Holly Farms
   Chicken Gizzards and
   Hearts
1/2 container Holly Farms
   Chicken Livers*
4 tablespoons butter or
   margarine
   salt and freshly ground
   pepper to taste
8 cups homemade chicken
   stock (page 24) or
   canned chicken broth

3/4 cup small pasta (bow ties,
   sea shells, etc.)
2 tablespoons freshly
   chopped parsley for
   garnish
   grated Parmesan or
   Romano cheese to
   serve

Place gizzards and hearts in lightly salted boiling water, cover, and cook 45 minutes or until tender. Drain, chop, and set aside. Rinse chicken livers under cold running water and pat dry with paper towels. Trim chicken livers and cut each liver into 4 pieces. Melt butter in skillet, add chicken livers, and sauté about 6 minutes or until livers are no longer pink. Remove from heat, season with salt and pepper, and set aside. Pour stock into large saucepan and bring to a boil. Add pasta and simmer 10 to 12 minutes or until pasta is cooked. Add reserved gizzards, hearts, and chicken livers, and simmer 2 to 3 minutes. Ladle into soup bowls, sprinkle with parsley, and serve with cheese.

TEXAS CHICKEN AND PEPPER SOUP

8 servings

- 1 Holly Farms Hen
- 1 large onion, cut into quarters
- 1 tablespoon salt
- 8 peppercorns
- 1 bouquet garni consisting of: 3 sprigs parsley, 1 bay leaf, and 1 or 2 sprigs thyme
- 1 red onion, cut into rings
- 1 green pepper, seeded and thinly sliced
- 1 red pepper, seeded and thinly sliced
- 1 can (16 ounces) chick peas, undrained
- 1 1/2 cups diced Monterey Jack cheese
- 1 avocado, peeled, pitted, and sliced
- 1 tablespoon lemon juice

Remove giblets and neck from chicken and rinse under cold running water. Place chicken, giblets, and neck in stockpot or large Dutch oven. Pour in 3 quarts cold water. Cover and bring to a boil. Skim surface of soup. Add quartered onion, salt, peppercorns, and bouquet garni. Simmer 3 hours, skimming surface and adding more water as necessary. Remove chicken and giblets with slotted spoon and set aside to cool. Strain broth, discarding bouquet garni, onion, and peppercorns. Return broth to clean saucepan. Remove and discard skin and bones from chicken. Cut meat and giblets into bite-size pieces and set aside. Bring broth to a boil. Add reserved chicken, giblets, onion rings, and green and red pepper slices. Simmer 10 minutes. Add chick peas, adjust seasoning, and simmer 5 minutes. Remove soup from heat and stir in cheese. Let stand 2 minutes or until cheese begins to melt. Ladle into soup bowls. Brush avocado slices with lemon juice and use to garnish soup. Serve with thick crusty French bread for a hearty lunch or light supper.

EASY CHICKEN NOODLE SOUP

4 to 6 servings

- 6 cups homemade chicken stock (page 24) or canned chicken broth
- 2 cups cubed cooked chicken (page 93)
- 2 cups egg noodles
- salt and freshly ground pepper to taste
- 1 tablespoon freshly chopped parsley for garnish

Place stock in large saucepan and bring to a boil slowly. Add chicken, noodles, salt, and pepper. Reduce heat and simmer 8 to 10 minutes or until noodles are cooked. Ladle into soup bowls and sprinkle with parsley.

Texas Chicken and Pepper Soup

CHICKEN CONSOMME

6 to 8 servings

8 cups homemade chicken
   stock (page 24)

2 egg whites
2 egg shells, crushed

Pour chicken stock into large saucepan. Beat egg whites slightly and add to stock with crushed egg shells. Bring stock to a simmer slowly without stirring. A thick crusty foam will form on top of stock. Do NOT skim surface. Simmer gently, uncovered, 15 minutes. Remove saucepan from heat carefully and cool 1 hour. Line large fine mesh strainer with double thickness of cheesecloth. Push foamy crust aside with spoon and ladle stock through lined strainer into large clean saucepan.

There are many ways to serve consommé:

I.   Reheat, adjust seasoning, and serve plain, sprinkled with freshly minced parsley.

II. Bring to a boil, add 1 1/2 cups thin egg noodles, reduce heat, and simmer 6 to 8 minutes or until noodles are cooked. Adjust seasoning and serve with grated Parmesan cheese if desired.

III. Serve with Toasted Croutons:
2 thick slices day-old white bread
6 tablespoons butter
1 clove garlic, crushed

Remove crusts from bread and cut bread into small cubes. Melt butter in skillet over moderate heat. Add garlic and cook 1 minute. Add bread cubes and sauté until golden brown, turning cubes several times to brown evenly on all sides. Remove bread cubes from skillet with slotted spoon and drain on paper towels. Serve on top of hot consommé, garnished with freshly minced parsley.

IV. Prepare any of the following recipes to go in consommé.

STRACCIATELLA

3 eggs
1/4 cup grated Parmesan
   cheese

8 cups consommé
1/8 teaspoon nutmeg
   (optional)

Beat eggs with fork. Add cheese and beat until well mixed. Bring consommé to a boil. Pour beaten egg mixture into consommé in slow, steady stream, stirring constantly with wire whisk. Reduce heat and simmer 3 to 4 minutes, stirring constantly. Add nutmeg, adjust seasoning, and serve immediately.

MATZO BALLS

3 eggs, separated
2 tablespoons chicken fat, melted (page 98)
1 teaspoon salt
freshly ground pepper to taste
3/4 cup matzo meal

1/4 teaspoon nutmeg (optional)
1 tablespoon freshly minced parsley (optional)
8 cups consommé

Beat egg yolks in large bowl until thick and lemon colored. Add chicken fat, salt and pepper, and mix well. Beat egg whites until stiff peaks form. Fold into egg yolk mixture. Add matzo meal, nutmeg, and parsley and fold gently. Cover and let stand at room temperature 10 minutes or, if time permits, refrigerate 1 hour or until ready to use. Wet hands and form mixture into 1 1/2-inch balls. Bring consommé to a boil. Drop matzo balls into boiling consommé. Reduce heat and cook 15 to 20 minutes or until matzo balls are cooked through.

POTATO-HERB DUMPLINGS

3 medium-size potatoes
1 egg, beaten
1/2 teaspoon salt
1/4 cup all-purpose flour
1 tablespoon freshly chopped parsley or 1 teaspoon dried parsley flakes

1 tablespoon minced onion or 1 teaspoon instant minced onion
8 cups consommé

Cooked unpeeled potatoes in lightly salted boiling water until tender. Drain and cool. When potatoes are cool enough to handle, peel and mash. Add beaten egg, salt, flour, parsley, and onion. Beat with fork or wire whisk until well mixed and fluffy. Flour hands and shape mixture into walnut-size balls. Bring consommé to a boil. Drop potato balls into boiling consommé, reduce heat, adjust seasoning, and simmer 10 to 12 minutes.

SPAETZLE

2 eggs
1/4 cup milk
1/2 teaspoon salt
1/8 teaspoon nutmeg

freshly ground pepper to taste
1 3/4 cups all-purpose flour
8 cups consommé

Beat eggs in large bowl. Add milk, 1/3 cup water, salt, nutmeg, and pepper. Blend well, add flour, and beat to make smooth batter. Bring consommé to a boil, reduce heat, adjust seasoning, and simmer. Pour batter into colander held over simmering consommé. Let batter drop through colander into hot consommé, pressing batter with back of wooden spoon as necessary. Simmer 10 to 12 minutes or until spaetzle is cooked through.

FAMILY CHICKEN SOUP
8 servings

1 Holly Farms Fryer or Hen
  salt and freshly ground
  pepper to taste
1 large onion, chopped
1 cup chopped celery
6 to 8 carrots, thickly
  sliced
2 parsnips, chopped
  (optional)
1/4 cup freshly chopped
  parsley
2 cups cooked rice or
  small pasta

Remove giblets and neck from chicken and rinse under cold running water. Place chicken, giblets, and neck in stockpot or large Dutch oven. Pour in 3 quarts cold water. Cover and bring to a boil slowly. Skim surface of soup. Lower heat, add salt and pepper, and simmer 1 1/2 hours, skimming surface as necessary. Remove chicken and giblets and set aside to cool. Line fine mesh strainer with double thickness of cheesecloth and strain broth. Return broth to stockpot. Add onion, celery, carrots, parsnips, parsley, salt, and pepper. Remove and discard skin and bones from chicken. Cut chicken and giblets into bite-size pieces and add to soup. Cover and simmer 25 to 30 minutes or until vegetables are tender. Add cooked rice or pasta to soup and simmer until heated through. Ladle into soup bowls and serve with crusty bread and grated Parmesan cheese if desired.

NOTE: You can use 6 to 8 cups homemade stock and about 3 cups cooked chicken from your freezer, adding vegetables and rice as directed above.

COCK-A-LEEKIE SOUP
6 to 8 servings

1 bunch leeks
3 tablespoons butter or
  margarine
1 large onion, chopped
8 cups homemade chicken
  stock (page 24) or
  canned chicken broth
1/2 teaspoon thyme
  salt and freshly ground
  pepper to taste
1/3 cup rice
2 1/2 cups cubed cooked
  chicken (page 93)

Rinse leeks under cold running water to remove sand. Remove any wilted outer leaves, trim ends, and thinly slice. Melt butter in large saucepan. Add leeks and onion and cook until onion is transparent. Add stock, thyme, salt, and pepper. Bring to a boil, add rice, cover, and cook over moderate heat 15 minutes. Add chicken, recover, and cook 5 to 10 minutes or until rice is just tender. Ladle into soup bowls and serve with hot biscuits or dinner rolls for a hearty meal.

COLD SENEGALESE SOUP
6 servings

4 cups homemade chicken stock (page 24) or canned chicken broth
1 1/2 cups diced cooked chicken (page 93)
2 teaspoons curry powder
salt and freshly ground pepper to taste

pinch cayenne
4 egg yolks
2 cups heavy cream
1 tablespoon snipped chives
chutney or thinly sliced apples for garnish

Place stock and diced chicken in large saucepan and bring to a boil slowly. Stir in curry powder, salt, pepper, and cayenne. Simmer 5 minutes. Beat egg yolks and cream in small bowl until blended. Slowly pour 1/2 cup hot stock into egg yolk mixture, beating constantly. Pour back into hot stock slowly, stirring constantly. Cook over low heat, stirring, until soup is slightly thickened. (Do not allow soup to boil or egg yolks will curdle.) Remove from heat and cool. Stir in chives and refrigerate several hours until well chilled. Ladle soup into bowls and garnish with chutney or apple slices.

CORN AND CHICKEN CHOWDER
4 to 6 servings

1 package Holly Farms Stripped Chicken Backs
1 package Holly Farms Chicken Gizzards and Hearts
1 onion, chopped
2 stalks celery, cut into chunks
salt and freshly ground pepper to taste

1 cup diced peeled potatoes
2 cups warm milk
1 can (17 ounces) whole kernel corn, drained
1/4 cup freshly chopped parsley for garnish

Place chicken backs, gizzards, hearts, onion, celery, salt, and pepper in stockpot or large Dutch oven. Add 6 cups cold water and bring to a boil slowly. Skim surface of soup. Add salt and pepper, cover, and simmer 1 1/2 hours, skimming surface as necessary. Strain broth, reserving chicken backs, gizzards, and hearts. Return broth to stockpot and bring to a boil. Add potatoes and simmer 10 minutes or until potatoes are just tender. Remove meat from chicken backs and add to soup. Chop gizzards and hearts and add to soup if desired. Add milk and corn, adjust seasoning, and simmer 5 minutes, stirring occasionally. Ladle into soup bowls, sprinkle with parsley, and serve with crackers or biscuits.

MULLIGATAWNY SOUP

4 to 6 servings

4 tablespoons butter or margarine
1 medium-size onion, finely chopped
1 carrot, diced
1 stalk celery, diced
3 tablespoons all-purpose flour
2 to 3 teaspoons curry powder
6 cups homemade chicken stock (page 24) or canned chicken broth
1 can (16 ounces) whole peeled tomatoes, chopped
1/4 teaspoon thyme
salt and freshly ground pepper to taste
1 1/2 cups cubed cooked chicken (page 93)
1 tart apple, peeled and diced
2 cups cooked rice

Melt butter in large saucepan. Add onion, carrot, and celery, and sauté until onion is transparent. Blend flour and curry powder and add to saucepan. Cook over moderate heat, stirring, until deep golden brown. Heat stock and add to saucepan with tomatoes, thyme, salt, and pepper. Stir well, cover, and simmer 20 minutes. Add chicken and apple and simmer 15 minutes. Stir in rice and simmer 5 minutes. Ladle into soup bowls and serve immediately.

ORIENTAL CHICKEN AND CUCUMBER SOUP

4 to 6 servings

6 cups homemade chicken stock (page 24) or canned chicken broth
2 tablespoons soy sauce
salt and freshly ground pepper to taste
2 Holly Farms Boneless Chicken Breasts
2 medium-size cucumbers, peeled and thinly sliced
2 tablespoons snipped chives for garnish

Place stock, soy sauce, salt, and pepper in large saucepan and bring to a boil. Add chicken breasts and simmer, covered, 10 to 12 minutes or until chicken is tender. Remove chicken with slotted spoon and cool. When cool enough to handle, shred chicken and return to stock. Return stock to a boil, reduce heat, add cucumber slices, and simmer 3 to 5 minutes or until cucumbers are almost soft. Sprinkle with chives. Ladle into soup bowls and serve immediately.

Roast Stuffed Chicken with Pan Gravy (page 34)

Main Dishes

ROAST STUFFED CHICKEN WITH PAN GRAVY

6 servings

1 **Holly Farms Roaster**
stuffing (see below)
salt and freshly ground
pepper to taste
paprika

Pan Gravy to serve
(see below)
Homemade Cooked
Cranberry Relish to
serve (see below)

Preheat oven to 350°F. Remove giblets from cavity of chicken and reserve to use in stuffing or gravy. Make stuffing (see below). Sprinkle neck and cavity of chicken with salt and pepper. Spoon stuffing lightly into neck and cavity. Do not pack tightly. Sew or truss cavity and neck to close (see page 94). Fold wing tips back and under upper part of wing. Place chicken, breast side up, on rack in roasting pan. Sprinkle all over with salt, pepper, and paprika. Roast, uncovered, 20 minutes per pound.

To test for doneness, pierce thickest part of thigh with fork. When juices run clear and drumstick moves easily in socket, chicken is done. A meat thermometer inserted in the thickest part of the thigh should register 180°F. Be sure tip of thermometer does not touch bone. To determine if stuffing is done, insert meat thermometer into center of stuffing. Thermometer should register 165°F. Remove chicken to carving board and let stand 15 to 20 minutes to firm meat before carving. Remove stuffing and place in serving bowl. Serve chicken with gravy, stuffing, and Homemade Cooked Cranberry Relish.

If chicken is to be roasted unstuffed, salt inside of cavity and roast as directed above. Reduce cooking time by about 15 minutes.

Cook giblets in lightly salted boiling water 1 hour or until tender. Drain, cool slightly, chop, and add to suffing or gravy.

Bread Stuffing:

4 **cups herb seasoned**
stuffing mix
1 **cup homemade chicken**
stock (page 24) or
canned chicken broth

1/2 **cup butter or margarine**
2 **eggs, lightly beaten**
optional ingredients
(see below)

Place stuffing mix in bowl. Set aside. Pour 1 cup stock into small saucepan. Add butter and bring to a boil. Cook until butter is melted. Pour over stuffing and mix well. Add beaten eggs and mix until well blended. Stir in any additional optional ingredients and stuff cavity and neck of chicken just before chicken is placed in oven.

Additions to stuffing: (Quantity depends on number of ingredients added to stuffing.)

chopped onion
sliced mushrooms
chopped cooked giblets
chopped celery

slivered almonds
chopped water chestnuts
chopped oysters
freshly chopped parsley

Rice and Nut Stuffing:

3 tablespoons butter or
   margarine
1 onion, chopped
1/2 cup diced celery
1 cup rice
2 1/2 cups homemade chicken
   stock (page 24) or
   canned chicken broth

2 tablespoons freshly
   chopped parsley
1 teaspoon poultry
   seasoning
1/4 cup toasted pine nuts
   (pignolia nuts) or
   1/2 cup toasted
   chopped almonds

Melt butter in medium-size saucepan. Add onion and celery and sauté until onion is transparent. Add rice and stir until rice is well coated. Add stock, parsley, and poultry seasoning. Stir well, bring to a boil, cover, and lower heat. Simmer 20 minutes or until all liquid has been absorbed. Add nuts and toss lightly. Stuff cavity and neck of chicken just before chicken is placed in oven.

NOTE: You will need 1/2 cup prepared stuffing per pound of chicken. Stuffing can be made ahead of time and refrigerated until needed. NEVER stuff chicken until you are ready to place it in oven. Remove stuffing from leftover chicken, cover, and refrigerate in separate dish.

Oyster Stuffing:

1 container (8 ounces)
   fresh oysters with
   liquor
2/3 cup butter or margarine
1 clove garlic, minced
1 onion, chopped
1/2 cup diced celery
4 cups dry bread cubes
   (see below)

1/4 cup freshly chopped
   parsley
1 teaspoon sage
1/2 teaspoon thyme
1/4 teaspoon nutmeg
   salt and freshly ground
   pepper to taste

Drain oysters, reserving liquor, and coarsely chop oysters. Melt butter in large saucepan. Add garlic, onion, and celery, and sauté until onion is transparent. Add oysters and sauté about 1 minute. Remove from heat. Add bread cubes, parsley, sage, thyme, nutmeg, reserved oyster liquor, salt, and pepper, and mix well. Stuff cavity and neck of chicken lightly just before chicken is placed in oven.

Pan Gravy:
about 2 cups

- 4 tablespoons pan drippings
- 4 tablespoons fat drippings
- 4 tablespoons all-purpose flour
- 2 cups homemade chicken stock (page 24) or canned chicken broth
- chopped cooked giblets (optional)
- 1/2 to 1 teaspoon browning sauce (optional)
- salt and freshly ground pepper to taste

Drain pan drippings and fat from roasting pan, separate, and set fat aside. Return pan drippings to roasting pan, add 2 tablespoons water, and scrape up browned particles over high heat. Reduce heat and stir in 4 tablespoons fat drippings. Add flour and stir to make smooth roux. Cook 2 minutes. Add stock slowly, stirring constantly, until gravy thickens. Add giblets, browning sauce, salt, and pepper, and stir well. Simmer until giblets are heated, pour into gravy boat, and serve with chicken.

Homemade Cooked Cranberry Relish:
about 2 cups

- 4 cups (1 pound) fresh cranberries
- 1 1/2 cups sugar
- 1 tablespoon grated orange rind
- 2 to 3 teaspoons lemon juice
- 1/2 cup chopped walnuts or slivered almonds
- 1/2 cup finely chopped celery

Wash cranberries, remove stems, and discard any shriveled or underripe berries. Place drained cranberries, sugar, and 1 cup water in saucepan. Stir well, bring to a boil, lower heat, and simmer 5 minutes or until skins begin to pop. Remove from heat and cool. Pour cranberries into bowl, add orange rind, lemon juice, walnuts, and celery, and mix well. Refrigerate until ready to serve.

Variation: To make Quick Cranberry Relish, omit cranberries and sugar. Use 1 can (16 ounces) whole berry cranberry sauce. Heat just until melted, cool slightly, stir in orange rind, lemon juice, walnuts, and celery. Refrigerate until ready to serve.

BATTER FRIED CHICKEN

6 servings

1 1/4 cups all-purpose flour
1 teaspoon salt
1 teaspoon baking powder
1/2 teaspoon thyme
 (optional)
1/4 teaspoon pepper
1 egg
3/4 cup milk
2 tablespoons vegetable oil

vegetable oil or
 shortening for frying
1 package Holly Farms
 Pick of the Chix or
 Best of the Fryer; or
 12 Prime Drumsticks or
 Prime Chicken Thighs

Combine flour, salt, baking powder, thyme, and pepper in medium-size bowl. Beat egg until frothy. Add milk and 2 tablespoons oil and beat until well blended. Pour into flour mixture and stir until well blended. Heat oil in deep-fat fryer or large skillet. Dip each chicken piece into batter and shake off excess. Carefully lower 3 or 4 chicken pieces into hot oil and deep-fry 10 to 15 minutes on each side, turning chicken with tongs. Fry until chicken is browned and tender. Remove chicken with tongs and drain on paper towels. Deep-fry remaining chicken pieces, 3 or 4 at a time.

Variation: Use self-rising flour, omit baking powder and salt, and proceed as directed above.

Beer Batter Fried Chicken: Use 1 cup all-purpose flour, 1 teaspoon salt, 1/4 teaspoon pepper, 1 tablespoon vegetable oil or melted butter, 1 egg, and 1/2 cup beer. Combine all ingredients and mix until well blended and smooth, or place ingredients in food processor or blender and process until smooth. Let batter stand at room temperature at least 4 hours before using. Add 1 stiffly beaten egg white to batter just before using if desired. Dip chicken into batter and deep-fry as directed above.

SOUTHERN FRIED CHICKEN   6 *servings*

3/4 cup all-purpose flour	vegetable oil or
1 1/2 teaspoons salt	shortening
1 teaspoon poultry	Cream Gravy (see below)
seasoning	to serve
1 to 2 teaspoons paprika	Buttermilk Biscuits
1/2 teaspoon pepper	(see below) to serve
1 egg, beaten with 1	
tablespoon water	
1 package Holly Farms	
Best of the Fryer, or	
Pick of the Chix, or	
Country Style Whole	
Chicken Cut Up	

Cover wire rack with waxed paper and set aside. Place flour, salt, poultry seasoning, paprika, and pepper in plastic bag. Cut breast pieces in half. Dip 1 chicken piece in egg and shake off excess. Place in plastic bag and shake to coat. Place coated chicken on rack. Repeat with remaining chicken. Let coated chicken stand on rack at least 15 minutes. Pour oil into 12-inch skillet to depth of 1 inch and heat. Add chicken and cook until browned on all sides, turning chicken frequently with tongs. Lower heat and cook 20 minutes or until chicken is tender. (Pieces of white meat will cook more quickly than dark meat.) Remove chicken with tongs and drain on paper towels. Reserve pan drippings to make Cream Gravy (below). Serve with gravy and Buttermilk Biscuits.

Cream Gravy: 2 *cups*

1/4 cup strained pan	1 cup light cream
drippings	salt and freshly ground
1/4 cup all-purpose flour	pepper to taste
1 cup homemade chicken	
stock (page 24) or	
canned chicken broth	

Heat pan drippings in saucepan until hot. Stir in flour and cook 1 minute. Add stock and cream slowly and cook over low heat, stirring constantly, until thickened and smooth. Season with salt and pepper. Pour gravy over fried chicken or serve separately in gravy boat.

Southern Fried Chicken

Buttermilk Biscuits
18 biscuits

2 cups all-purpose flour	1 teaspoon salt
2 teaspoons baking powder	5 tablespoons shortening
1/4 teaspoon baking soda	3/4 cup buttermilk

Preheat oven to 450°F. Stir flour, baking powder, baking soda, and salt in bowl. Cut in shortening with pastry blender or 2 knives until mixture resembles coarse crumbs. Make well in center, add buttermilk, and mix with fork until dough is soft and holds together. Place dough on lightly floured surface and knead about 10 strokes. Roll out dough to 1/2-inch thickness and cut into rounds with floured 2-inch biscuit cutter. Gather dough scraps, reroll, and cut. Lift biscuits with flat spatula and place on ungreased cookie sheet, spacing them 1 inch apart for crusty biscuits or close together for soft biscuits. Bake 12 to 15 minutes or until golden brown. Remove from cookie sheet immediately and serve piping hot.

Variation: Baking Powder Biscuits: Omit baking soda and increase baking powder to 1 tablespoon. Use whole milk instead of buttermilk. Proceed as directed above.

OVEN FRIED CHICKEN
6 servings

1/4 cup crushed stuffing mix	1/4 teaspoon pepper
1/4 cup cornflake crumbs	1 package Holly Farms Pick
1/4 cup all-purpose flour	of the Chix, Best of the
1 teaspoon garlic powder	Fryer, or Country Style
or onion powder	Whole Chicken Cut Up
1 teaspoon paprika	3 to 4 tablespoons melted
1/2 teaspoon Italian	butter, margarine, or
seasoning	vegetable oil
1/2 teaspoon salt	

Preheat oven to 375°F. Combine stuffing mix, cornflake crumbs, flour, garlic powder, paprika, Italian seasoning, salt, and pepper, and place in shallow dish. Brush chicken pieces with melted butter and roll in coating mixture. Arrange coated chicken in single layer in roasting pan and bake 30 minutes. Turn chicken pieces over and bake 30 minutes or until tender. Arrange on serving platter and serve hot.

Microwave Method: Prepare chicken as directed above. Arrange coated chicken in shallow microproof dish, placing thickest portions of chicken at outer edge of dish. Cover with paper towel and microcook at 100% power 10 minutes. Turn chicken over, recover, and microcook at 100% power 10 to 12 minutes until chicken is tender.

CHICKEN FRICASSEE WITH DILL SAUCE

4 to 6 servings

1 package Holly Farms
   Country Style Whole
   Chicken Cut Up or
   1 package Pick of
   the Chix
salt and freshly ground
   pepper to taste
3 tablespoons vegetable
   oil
3 cups homemade hot
   chicken stock (page 24)
   or canned chicken broth
1 large onion, cut into
   quarters

1 carrot, cut into chunks
1 stalk celery with leaves
3 sprigs parsley
1 bay leaf
5 tablespoons butter or
   margarine, divided
1/2 pound mushrooms, sliced
3 tablespoons all-purpose
   flour
2 egg yolks
1/2 cup heavy cream
1/3 cup freshly chopped dill
   or 1 to 2 tablespoons
   dried dill

Season chicken with salt and pepper. Heat oil in Dutch oven. Add chicken pieces and brown well on all sides. Add stock, onion, carrot, celery, parsley, and bay leaf, and bring to a boil. Lower heat, cover, and simmer 40 to 45 minutes or until chicken is tender. Remove chicken with slotted spoon and set aside. Strain stock, discarding vegetables and bay leaf. Set stock aside. Melt 2 tablespoons butter in skillet. Add mushrooms and sauté about 5 minutes. Remove from heat and set aside. Melt remaining 3 tablespoons butter in Dutch oven. Add flour and cook, stirring, 1 minute. Add reserved stock slowly and cook, stirring constantly, until sauce is thickened and comes to a boil. Beat egg yolks and cream in small bowl. Add a little hot sauce to beaten egg yolk mixture and stir until blended. Pour egg yolk mixture back into sauce and stir well. Add reserved chicken pieces, mushrooms, and dill, and cook over low heat, stirring occasionally, until chicken is heated through.

BARBECUED CHICKEN PERFECTION

8 servings

2 packages Holly Farms
Split Chicken, or
2 packages Whole
Chicken Quartered, or
8 Prime Chicken
Breast Quarters, or
8 Prime Chicken Leg
Quarters, or 8 Prime
Breast Halves

Barbecue Sauces (see
below) or 1 jar
(16 ounces) barbecue
sauce

Place chicken on grill, skin side down, about 5 to 6 inches from source of heat. Grill over medium-hot coals 35 minutes, turning chicken occasionally with tongs. Keep saucepan of barbecue sauce on side of grill to keep warm. Brush chicken with barbecue sauce and grill 20 to 25 minutes or until chicken is tender, turning and brushing chicken with sauce frequently. Serve with a good supply of napkins.

TIP: Chicken may be precooked in the microwave oven at 100% power 7 to 8 minutes, and then barbecued as directed above.

Barbecue Sauce I

about 2 cups

2 tablespoons vegetable
oil
1 cup finely minced
onions
1 cup ketchup
1/4 cup cider vinegar
1/3 cup firmly packed brown
sugar

2 tablespoons Worcester-
shire sauce
2 teaspoons dry mustard
2 teaspoons liquid smoke
(optional)
1 to 2 teaspoons salt
1/4 teaspoon hot pepper
sauce or to taste

Heat oil in saucepan with flameproof handle. Add onions and sauté until onions are transparent. Add ketchup, vinegar, 1/4 cup water, brown sugar, Worcestershire, mustard, liquid smoke, salt, and hot pepper sauce. Stir well and bring to a boil. Lower heat and simmer 5 to 7 minutes, stirring occasionally. Brush over chicken.

Barbecued Chicken Perfection

Barbecue Sauce II
about 2 1/2 cups

2 tablespoons vegetable oil
1/2 cup minced onion
1 large clove garlic, minced
1 can (8 ounces) tomato sauce
1 cup prepared chili sauce

2 tablespoons cider vinegar
1 tablespoon lemon juice
2 tablespoons sugar
2 teaspoons chili powder
1 teaspoon dry mustard

Heat oil in medium-size saucepan with flameproof handle. Add onion and garlic and sauté until onion is transparent. Add tomato sauce, chili sauce, vinegar, lemon juice, sugar, chili powder, and mustard. Stir well and bring to a boil. Lower heat and simmer 10 to 12 minutes, stirring occasionally. Brush over chicken.

Variation: Omit chili sauce. Use 1 can (10 ounces) enchilada sauce.

Blue Ridge Barbecue Sauce
about 2 cups

1 1/2 cups cider vinegar
3/4 cup vegetable oil
3 tablespoons lemon juice
2 tablespoons chili powder
2 teaspoons garlic powder

3/4 teaspoon cayenne or to taste
salt and freshly ground pepper to taste

Combine vinegar, oil, lemon juice, chili powder, garlic powder, cayenne, salt, and pepper in medium-size saucepan with flameproof handle. Stir until well blended. Place over low heat and bring to a boil slowly. Simmer, uncovered, 5 to 7 minutes, stirring occasionally. Brush over chicken.

CRISPY BAKED DRUMSTICKS
6 servings

about 1/3 cup all-purpose flour
freshly ground pepper to taste
2 cups crushed potato chips (plain, sour cream and onion, or barbecue flavored)

12 to 14 Holly Farms Prime Chicken Drumsticks
1 egg beaten with 1 tablespoon water
1/4 cup butter or margarine

Cover wire rack with waxed paper and set aside. Place flour on large piece of waxed paper and season with pepper. Spread potato chips on separate piece of waxed paper. Dredge 1 drumstick in flour, dip in beaten egg, shaking off excess, and roll in potato chips until thoroughly coated. Place coated drumstick on covered wire rack. Repeat with remaining drumsticks. Refrigerate 1 hour. Preheat oven to 375°F. Place butter in baking pan large enough to hold drumsticks in single layer and place pan in oven until butter is melted. Remove pan from oven and arrange drumsticks in pan. Bake 45 to 50 minutes or until chicken is tender, basting and turning once or twice during cooking. Serve hot, or cool completely and take along on a picnic.

CHICKEN AND OLIVES ITALIANO

4 to 6 servings

1/4 cup vegetable oil
1 package Holly Farms Best of the Fryer or Pick of the Chix
1 cup chopped onions
1 cup chopped celery
2 medium-size ripe tomatoes, peeled and chopped, or 1 cup canned tomatoes, chopped

1 cup homemade chicken stock (page 24) or canned chicken broth
1 tablespoon red wine vinegar
1 tablespoon drained capers (optional)
12 jumbo pitted green olives, cut in half
salt and freshly ground pepper to taste

Preheat oven to 350°F. Heat oil in large skillet. Add chicken and brown well on all sides. Remove chicken with tongs to deep 3-quart casserole. Add onions, celery, tomatoes, stock, vinegar, capers, olives, salt, and pepper, and mix well. Cover and bake 1 hour to 1 hour 15 minutes or until chicken is tender.

Hint: This tastes best when prepared a day in advance to allow time for flavors to blend. Reheat in 350°F oven 20 to 25 minutes or until heated through.

Microwave Method: Brown chicken in skillet as directed above. Add remaining ingredients to skillet, reducing stock to 1/2 cup. Bring to a boil and remove from heat. Arrange chicken in single layer in 3-quart microproof baking dish, placing thickest part of chicken at outer edge of dish. Pour tomato mixture over, cover loosely, and microcook at 100% power 18 to 22 minutes, turning chicken and basting once during cooking. Let stand 5 minutes.

PAELLA VALENCIANA

6 to 8 servings

1 package Holly Farms
   Pick of the Chix or
   Best of the Fryer
salt and freshly ground
   pepper to taste
about 1/3 cup all-
   purpose flour
1/2 cup olive oil
2 cloves garlic, minced
2 large onions, chopped
1 green or red pepper,
   seeded and chopped
1 1/2 cups rice
1 can (16 ounces) whole
   peeled tomatoes,
   drained
1/2 teaspoon thyme
1/2 teaspoon oregano
1/4 teaspoon ground saffron
   or a few saffron
   threads

1/4 teaspoon ground cumin
1 bay leaf
3 cups homemade chicken
   stock (page 24) or
   canned chicken broth
3/4 cup dry white wine
12 to 16 medium-size shrimp,
   shelled and deveined
1 package (10 ounces)
   frozen artichoke
   hearts or tiny peas,
   thawed
8 to 12 cherrystone or
   littleneck clams,
   scrubbed
1 jar (4 ounces) sliced
   pimientos, drained,
   for garnish

Season chicken with salt and pepper. Place flour in plastic bag, add 1 or 2 chicken pieces, and shake to coat. Set coated chicken aside and repeat with remaining chicken. Heat oil in large flame proof casserole, Dutch oven, or paella pan. Add chicken and brown well on all sides. Remove chicken with tongs and set aside. Preheat oven to 375°F. Add garlic, onions, and green pepper to casserole, and sauté until onion is transparent. Add rice, tomatoes, thyme, oregano, saffron, cumin, bay leaf, salt, and pepper, and stir well. Add stock and wine and bring to a boil. Return chicken to casserole, spooning rice mixture over chicken. Remove casserole from heat, cover, and bake 40 minutes. Add shrimp. Push shrimp down into rice mixture, add artichoke hearts, and arrange clams on top. Recover and bake 10 minutes. Uncover and bake 5 to 10 minutes or until clams have opened and rice has absorbed all liquid. Remove and discard bay leaf, and garnish with pimientos.

Variation: Substitute 1 cup clam juice for part of the chicken stock. If you own a paella pan, you can cook this dish on top of the range.

STUFFED BREASTS SORRENTINO *6 to 8 servings*

8 Holly Farms Boneless Chicken Breasts or 12 to 16 Boneless Chicken Thigh Fillets
salt, freshly ground pepper, and paprika to taste
6 tablespoons butter or margarine, divided
1 medium-size onion, minced
1/2 pound mushrooms, chopped
1 package (10 ounces) frozen chopped spinach, thawed and well drained
1 cup small curd creamy-style cottage cheese or ricotta cheese
1 egg, beaten
1/2 teaspoon Italian seasoning
1/4 teaspoon nutmeg
3/4 cup grated Romano or Parmesan cheese, divided
1/2 cup dry white wine
parsley sprigs for garnish

Make pocket in each chicken breast and season all over with salt, pepper, and paprika. Set aside. Melt 4 tablespoons butter in skillet. Add onion and mushrooms and sauté until onion is transparent. Add spinach, stir well, and simmer until all moisture has evaporated. Remove skillet from heat, and add cottage cheese, beaten egg, Italian seasoning, nutmeg, salt, pepper, and 1/2 cup grated Romano cheese. Stir until thoroughly combined. Preheat oven to 350°F. Spoon 2 to 3 tablespoons spinach filling into each chicken pocket. Fold chicken over to enclose filling. Place chicken, seam side down, in single layer in greased shallow baking dish. Melt remaining 2 tablespoons butter and brush over chicken. Pour wine into bottom of dish. Bake 25 minutes, basting with pan juices several times. Sprinkle remaining 1/4 cup Romano cheese over chicken and bake 10 to 15 minutes or until cheese is melted and chicken is tender. Arrange on serving platter and garnish with parsley.

NOTE: Chicken breasts will cook more quickly than thigh fillets.

CHICKEN CACCIATORE

6 servings

1/2 cup all-purpose flour
  salt and freshly ground
    pepper to taste
1 teaspoon paprika
1 package Holly Farms
    Pick of the Chix or
    Best of the Fryer
2 tablespoons olive oil
2 tablespoons vegetable
    oil
1 onion, chopped
2 cloves garlic, very
    thinly sliced

1 green pepper, seeded
    and coarsely chopped
1 can (16 ounces) whole
    peeled plum tomatoes
1/2 cup dry red wine
2 tablespoons freshly
    chopped parsley
1 bay leaf
1 1/2 teaspoons Italian
    seasoning
  hot cooked spaghetti
    to serve

Place flour, salt, pepper, and paprika in plastic bag. Add 1 chicken piece and shake to coat. Set coated chicken aside and repeat with remaining chicken. Heat oils in large skillet, add chicken, and brown well on all sides. Remove chicken with tongs and set aside. Add onion, garlic, and green pepper to skillet and sauté until onion is transparent. Add tomatoes, parsley, bay leaf, Italian seasoning, salt, pepper, and wine, and stir well. Slowly bring to a boil. Return chicken to skillet and spoon sauce over chicken. Cover and simmer 40 to 50 minutes or until chicken is tender, stirring occasionally and turning chicken during cooking. Uncover, skim surface of sauce, and remove and discard bay leaf. Serve with hot cooked spaghetti.

Microwave Method: Coat chicken with flour and brown as directed above. Arrange chicken in shallow 2-quart microproof casserole, placing thickest part of chicken pieces at outer edge of dish. Prepare sauce as directed above, reducing wine to 1/4 cup. Pour over chicken, cover and microcook at 100% power 10 minutes. Uncover and turn chicken pieces over. Recover and microcook at 100% power 8 to 10 minutes or until chicken is tender. Serve as directed above.

Chicken Cacciatore, Chicken Thighs
Mozzarella (pages 50, 51)

CHICKEN NORMANDY

6 servings

1 package Holly Farms Pick of the Chix or Best of the Fryer

salt and freshly ground pepper to taste

3 tablespoons butter or margarine

2 tablespoons vegetable oil

1 onion, thinly sliced

2 tart apples, peeled, cored, and diced

1/2 cup diced celery

2 tablespoons all-purpose flour

1 cup apple cider or applejack

1/2 cup homemade chicken stock (page 24) or canned chicken broth

1/2 cup heavy cream

4 slices bacon, cooked and crumbled for garnish (optional)

Season chicken with salt and pepper. Heat butter and oil in Dutch oven. Add chicken and brown well on all sides. Remove chicken with tongs and set aside. Add onion to pan and sauté until transparent. Add apples and celery and sauté 3 minutes. Sprinkle flour over apple-onion mixture and cook, stirring, 2 minutes. Gradually add apple cider and stock and cook, stirring, until mixture comes to a boil. Return chicken to pan, lower heat, cover, and simmer 40 to 50 minutes or until chicken is tender. Adjust seasoning, add cream, and cook, stirring, until sauce is thickened and comes to a boil. Arrange chicken on serving platter, spoon sauce over, and sprinkle with bacon.

CHICKEN THIGHS MOZZARELLA

4 servings

6 to 8 Holly Farms Boneless Chicken Thigh Fillets

1/3 cup all-purpose flour

2 tablespoons grated Parmesan cheese

salt and freshly ground pepper to taste

1 egg beaten with 1 tablespoon water

2 tablespoons vegetable oil

4 to 6 tablespoons butter or margarine, divided

3/4 pound mushrooms, sliced

3 to 4 slices cooked ham

6 to 8 slices mozzarella cheese

finely chopped fresh parsley for garnish (optional)

Place each thigh between 2 sheets of plastic wrap and pound with meat mallet or rolling pin to flatten. Combine flour, Parmesan cheese, salt, and pepper. Dip each thigh in beaten egg, shake off excess, and dredge in flour mixture. Heat oil and 2 to 4 tablespoons butter in skillet. Add coated thighs and cook

2 minutes on each side or until golden brown. Remove thighs with slotted spoon and arrange in single layer in 12×8-inch baking dish. Preheat oven to 350°F. Bake 35 to 40 minutes or until chicken is tender. Add remaining 2 tablespoons butter to skillet and sauté mushrooms 4 minutes. Scatter mushrooms over chicken. Cut each ham slice in half and place 1/2 ham slice and 1 slice mozzarella over each thigh. Broil just until cheese is melted and lightly browned. Sprinkle with parsley and serve immediately.

Microwave Method: Prepare as directed above but do not add mozzarella. Cover loosely with plastic wrap. Microcook at 100% power 9 minutes. Add mozzarella, recover, and microcook at 100% power 3 minutes or until chicken is tender.

CHICKEN SCALLOPINE

6 to 8 servings

8 Holly Farms Boneless
   Chicken Breasts or
   12 to 16 Boneless
   Chicken Thigh Fillets
   salt and freshly ground
   pepper to taste
1/4 cup all-purpose flour
7 tablespoons butter or
   margarine, divided
3/4 pound mushrooms, sliced
2 teaspoons lemon juice
2 tablespoons vegetable
   oil

1/4 pound prosciutto or
   Westphalian ham, cut
   into thin strips
1/2 cup marsala or dry
   sherry
1/2 cup homemade chicken
   stock (page 24) or
   canned chicken broth
2 tablespoons freshly
   chopped parsley for
   garnish

Place chicken breasts, 1 at a time, between 2 sheets of plastic wrap and pound with meat mallet or rolling pin to flatten. Season with salt and pepper. Place flour on flat plate. Dredge chicken breasts in flour, shaking off excess. Melt 3 tablespoons butter in skillet. Add mushrooms and sauté about 5 minutes. Remove mushrooms with slotted spoon, sprinkle with lemon juice, and set aside. Melt remaining 4 tablespoons butter and oil in skillet. Add chicken breasts and sauté until lightly browned on both sides. Remove breasts and keep warm. Add prosciutto to skillet and sauté until brown. Add marsala and stock and bring to a boil, scraping up brown particles in skillet. Boil rapidly 2 minutes. Return chicken and mushrooms to skillet, lower heat, and simmer 3 to 5 minutes or until chicken is tender. Arrange chicken on serving platter. Spoon mushrooms and prosciutto on top of chicken. Bring sauce in skillet to a boil and boil rapidly until reduced by one-third. Pour sauce over chicken, sprinkle with parsley, and serve immediately.

ROSEMARY CHICKEN en COCOTTE   6 *servings*

1 Holly Farms Roaster
  salt and freshly ground
  pepper to taste
1 large onion, cut into
  quarters
2 cloves garlic
1 small stalk celery with
  leaves
1 small carrot
6 sprigs fresh rosemary
  or 1 teaspoon dried
  rosemary
paprika
juice of 1 large lemon

Remove giblets from chicken and reserve for use another time. Preheat oven to 450°F. Season cavity with salt and pepper. Place onion, garlic, celery, carrot, and 2 sprigs rosemary in cavity of chicken. Close cavity with small metal skewers or poultry lacers. Secure neck to back of chicken with small metal skewer. Tuck wing tips under upper part of chicken. Wrap kitchen string around breast and wings and tie securely. Season chicken all over with salt, pepper, and paprika. Place chicken in clay pot (chicken should fit snugly). Place remaining rosemary sprigs over chicken and sprinkle chicken with lemon juice. Cover with ceramic top and bake 1 hour 20 minutes to 1 hour 30 minutes or until chicken is tender. Do not remove cover during cooking. To serve, remove chicken from pot, untie string, and remove skewers. Remove and discard vegetables in cavity and place chicken on carving board.

CHICKEN BREASTS TOUSSAINT   4 *servings*

4 Holly Farms Country
  Style Chicken Breasts
  or Prime Chicken
  Breast Halves
1 envelope dehydrated
  onion soup mix
1 can (6 ounces) frozen
  concentrated orange
  juice, undiluted and thawed
1 can (11 ounces) mandarin
  oranges, drained and
  liquid reserved
2 tablespoons orange-
  flavored liqueur
  (optional)
toasted slivered almonds

Preheat oven to 350°F. Arrange chicken, skin side up, in shallow casserole. Sprinkle onion soup mix over chicken. Combine orange juice with reserved liquid from oranges, mix thoroughly, and pour over chicken. Sprinkle liqueur over chicken. Bake 30 minutes, basting chicken occasionally with pan juices. Remove from oven and arrange mandarin oranges over chicken. Return to oven and bake 15 minutes. Scatter almonds over chicken just before serving.

Microwave Method: Brush skin of chicken with browning sauce. Arrange chicken in shallow microproof baking dish, placing thickest part of chicken at outer edge of dish. Sprinkle onion soup mix over chicken. Combine orange juice with 1/4 cup reserved liquid from oranges, mix thoroughly, and pour over chicken. Sprinkle liqueur over chicken, cover loosely, and microcook at 100% power 8 minutes. Baste chicken with sauce, recover, and microcook at 100% power 8 minutes. Arrange mandarin oranges over chicken, recover, and microcook at 100% power 3 to 4 minutes or until chicken is tender. Let stand, covered, 5 minutes. Scatter almonds over chicken just before serving.

CHICKEN MARENGO
4 to 6 servings

1 package Holly Farms Pick of the Chix, Best of the Fryer, or Country Style Whole Chicken Cut Up
salt, freshly ground pepper, and paprika to taste
1/3 cup all-purpose flour
1/4 cup olive oil or vegetable oil
1 large clove garlic, minced
1 large onion, minced
1/2 pound mushrooms, sliced
1 can (16 ounces) whole peeled tomatoes
1 cup dry white wine
1/2 cup homemade chicken stock (page 24) or canned chicken broth
2 tablespoons tomato paste
1/2 teaspoon thyme
12 to 16 pimiento stuffed green olives or pitted ripe olives
toast points to serve
2 tablespoons freshly chopped parsley for garnish

Season chicken with salt, pepper, and paprika. Place flour in plastic bag. Add 1 or 2 chicken pieces and shake to coat. Set coated chicken aside and repeat with remaining chicken. Heat oil in Dutch oven or deep flameproof casserole. Add chicken and brown well on all sides. Remove with tongs and set aside. Add garlic, onion, and mushrooms, and sauté until onion is transparent. Add tomatoes, wine, stock, tomato paste, thyme, salt, and pepper. Break up tomatoes with back of spoon and bring to a boil, stirring. Return chicken to pan and spoon tomato mixture over chicken. Lower heat, cover, and simmer 40 to 45 minutes or until chicken is tender. Stir in olives. Arrange chicken on warm serving platter, surround with toast points, spoon sauce over, and garnish with parsley.

Microwave Method: Brown chicken and prepare sauce as directed above. Arrange browned chicken pieces in 3-quart microproof casserole, placing thickest part of chicken pieces at outer edge of dish. Pour sauce over, cover lightly, and micro-cook at 100% power 22 to 25 minutes, stirring after 15 minutes. Let stand 10 minutes before serving. Serve as directed above.

SUPREMES OF CHICKEN
6 servings

- 12 to 16 small mushroom caps for garnish
- 6 tablespoons butter or margarine, divided
- Sauce Supreme (see below)
- 6 to 8 Holly Farms Boneless Chicken Breasts
- salt and freshly ground pepper to taste
- 1/2 cup homemade chicken stock (page 24) or canned chicken broth orange, thinly sliced, sprigs of watercress or parsley for garnish

Sauté mushrooms in 2 tablespoons butter, set aside and keep warm. Make Sauce Supreme and set aside. Place chicken breasts, 1 at a time, between 2 sheets of waxed paper and pound with meat mallet or rolling pin to flatten. Season chicken breasts with salt and pepper. Melt remaining 4 tablespoons butter in skillet. Add chicken breasts and sauté until golden on both sides. Add stock, cover, lower heat, and poach 10 to 12 minutes or until tender. Turn breasts once or twice during cooking. Remove to warm serving platter. Reheat sauce if necessary, pour over chicken and garnish with mushroom caps, thin slices of orange, and watercress. Serve immediately.

SAUCE SUPREME:

- 2 cups homemade chicken stock (page 24) or canned chicken broth
- 1/4 cup dry white wine or dry sherry
- 2 tablespoons butter or margarine
- 2 tablespoons all-purpose flour
- salt and white pepper to taste
- 1/8 teaspoon nutmeg
- 1/2 cup heavy cream

Place stock and wine in saucepan and bring to a boil. Boil rapidly until liquid is reduced to 1 cup. Set aside. Melt butter in saucepan. Add flour and cook, stirring, 1 minute. Add reserved chicken stock and wine mixture and cook, stirring constantly, until sauce is thickened and smooth. Season with salt, pepper, and nutmeg. Stir in cream and simmer 3 minutes, stirring occasionally. Pour sauce over chicken breasts.

Supremes of Chicken, Chicken Thighs Cordon Bleu (page 56)

CHICKEN THIGHS CORDON BLEU *4 servings*

8 Holly Farms Boneless
  Chicken Thigh Fillets
1/4 cup all-purpose flour
  salt, freshly ground
  pepper and paprika to
  taste
4 slices Swiss cheese
4 thin slices cooked ham
1 egg beaten with 1
  tablespoon water
4 tablespoons butter or
  margarine

2 tablespoons dry sherry
  (optional)
1/2 cup homemade chicken
  stock (page 24) or
  canned chicken broth
2 teaspoons cornstarch
3/4 cup light cream or half
  and half
2 tablespoons freshly
  chopped parsley

Place each thigh fillet between 2 sheets of plastic wrap and pound with meat mallet or rolling pin to flatten slightly. Combine flour, salt, pepper, and paprika in shallow dish. Set aside. Cut each ham slice and each cheese slice in half. Fold 1/2 ham slice and 1/2 cheese slice together and place in center of 1 thigh fillet. Fold thigh fillet around ham and cheese to enclose completely, and secure with wooden toothpick. Repeat with remaining thighs, ham, and cheese. Dip stuffed thighs in beaten egg, shake off excess, and dredge in flour mixture. Melt butter in skillet. Add stuffed thighs and sauté until browned on all sides. Add sherry and stock to skillet and bring to a boil. Cover, lower heat, and simmer 30 to 35 minutes or until chicken is tender. Remove chicken from skillet, remove and discard toothpicks, and arrange on warm serving platter. Blend cornstarch with cream, stirring until smooth. Gradually stir into skillet with pan juices and cook over low heat, stirring constantly, until sauce is thickened and comes to a boil. Stir in parsley. Pour sauce into gravy boat and serve with chicken.

Microwave Method: Prepare, stuff, and brown thighs as directed above. Arrange thighs in circular fashion in 9-inch round microproof baking dish. Pour in sherry and 1/4 cup chicken stock. Cover loosely with plastic wrap. Microcook at 50% power 10 to 12 minutes or until chicken is tender. Remove chicken to serving platter and discard toothpicks. Pour pan juices into 2-cup glass measure. Add cornstarch and cream and stir until cornstarch is dissolved. Microcook at 100% power 3 to 4 minutes or until sauce is thickened and comes to a boil, stirring after each minute. Stir in parsley and pour sauce into gravy boat. Serve with chicken.

CHICKEN VERONIQUE

6 servings

6 Holly Farms Prime
   Chicken Breast Halves
   salt, freshly ground
   pepper, and paprika
   to taste
6 tablespoons butter or
   margarine, divided
1 clove garlic, minced
1 onion, minced
1 cup homemade chicken
   stock (page 24) or
   canned chicken broth

1/2 cup dry white wine
2 tablespoons lemon juice
1/2 pound large mushrooms,
   cut into quarters
1 tablespoon cornstarch
1 to 1 1/2 cups seedless
   green grapes

Season chicken breasts with salt, pepper, and paprika. Melt 4 tablespoons butter in large skillet. Add breasts and brown well on all sides. Remove from skillet and set aside. Add garlic and onion to skillet and sauté until onion is transparent. Add stock, wine, and lemon juice, and bring to a boil. Return chicken to skillet and spoon sauce over chicken. Cover and simmer 30 to 35 minutes or until chicken is tender. Melt remaining 2 table-spoons butter in separate small skillet and sauté mushrooms until lightly browned. Set aside and keep warm. Remove chicken from skillet with tongs and set aside. Skim fat from pan juices. Dissolve cornstarch in 2 tablespoons water and stir into pan juices. Cook over low heat, stirring constantly, until sauce is thickened. Return chicken to skillet, spooning sauce over. Add grapes and simmer 3 to 5 minutes or until heated through. Arrange chicken breasts on serving platter, spoon sauce over, and garnish with reserved mushrooms.

CHINESE CHICKEN WITH PEA PODS

4 to 6 servings

6 to 8 Holly Farms Boneless Chicken Thigh Fillets or 4 Boneless Chicken Breasts
3 tablespoons soy sauce
2 cloves garlic, minced
1/2 teaspoon ground ginger
2 to 3 tablespoons peanut oil
2 stalks celery, cut into 2-inch strips
1 bunch scallions, cut into 2-inch lengths (green tops included)

1/2 pound Chinese pea pods or 1 package (6 ounces) frozen Chinese pea pods, thawed
1 cup homemade chicken stock (page 24) or canned chicken broth, divided
1 jar (6 ounces) sliced mushrooms, drained
1 tablespoon cornstarch
2 teaspoons sesame oil (optional)
hot cooked rice to serve

Cut chicken into cubes or thin strips and place in bowl. Blend soy sauce, garlic, and ginger, and pour over chicken. Mix until chicken is well coated. Heat peanut oil in wok or large skillet. Add chicken and any liquid remaining in bowl. Stir-fry over high heat until chicken is lightly browned. Remove chicken with slotted spoon and keep warm. Add celery and stir-fry 2 minutes. Push to one side, add scallions, and stir-fry 1 minute. Add pea pods, reserved chicken, and 1/2 cup stock. Cover and cook 5 minutes or until pea pods are just crisp. Add mushrooms. Blend cornstarch with remaining 1/2 cup stock and add to wok. Cook, stirring until sauce is thickened. Sprinkle with sesame oil and serve immediately with hot cooked rice.

Microwave Method: Place 2 tablespoons peanut oil, celery, and scallions in 2-quart microproof baking dish. Cover loosely and microcook at 100% power 2 minutes. Cut chicken into cubes and mix with soy sauce, garlic, and ginger. Add to celery mixture and stir well. Add pea pods and mushrooms and stir. Blend cornstarch with 1/2 cup stock, stirring until cornstarch is dissolved. Add to chicken mixture and stir well. Recover and microcook at 100% power 8 to 9 minutes, stirring twice during cooking. Serve as directed above.

Chinese Chicken With Pea Pods

TERIYAKI CHICKEN
4 servings

1/4 cup soy sauce
1/4 cup dry sherry or sake
1 tablespoon brown sugar
1 tablespoon freshly minced gingerroot or 1 teaspoon ground ginger
1 large clove garlic, minced
4 slices lemon, chopped, or 2 tablespoons lemon juice
2 tablespoons minced onion
1 package Holly Farms Whole Chicken Quartered, or Split Chicken, or 8 Prime Chicken Thighs, or 4 Prime Chicken Breast Halves
lemon wedges for garnish

Combine soy sauce, sherry, brown sugar, gingerroot, garlic, lemon, and onion, stirring until well blended. Arrange chicken in single layer in shallow glass baking dish. Pour marinade over and turn to coat well. Cover and refrigerate at least 4 hours, turning chicken occasionally. Preheat oven to 325°F. Uncover chicken and bake in marinade 1 hour to 1 hour 15 minutes or until chicken is tender, basting several times with marinade. Arrange chicken on warm serving platter and garnish with lemon wedges.

Microwave Method: Prepare and marinate chicken as directed above. Arrange chicken in single layer in shallow microproof baking dish, placing thickest part of chicken pieces at outer edge of dish. Cover loosely with plastic wrap. Micro-cook at 100% power 24 to 28 minutes or until chicken is tender, basting chicken with marinade 3 or 4 times during cooking.

SZECHUAN-STYLE CHICKEN
4 to 6 servings

2 Holly Farms Whole Chicken Breasts or 4 Chicken Breast Halves
2 tablespoons soy sauce
1 teaspoon chili paste with garlic*
5 tablespoons peanut oil, divided
1 tablespoon cornstarch
1/4 cup thinly sliced scallions
1/2 cup unsalted peanuts
1 tablespoon finely chopped fresh gingerroot or 1 teaspoon ground ginger
2 teaspoons white or cider vinegar
1 tablespoon dry sherry
1/2 teaspoon sesame oil (optional)

Split breasts in half, and remove skin and bones. Cut chicken into 2-inch long strips. Combine soy sauce, chili paste, 1 table-spoon peanut oil, and cornstarch. Stir until well mixed. Place chicken and scallions in bowl. Add soy sauce mixture and stir until chicken strips are coated. Heat remaining 4 tablespoons peanut oil in wok or large skillet. Add peanuts and stir-fry over high heat just until golden. Add chicken-scallion mixture to wok and stir-fry 2 minutes. Mix ginger, vinegar, sherry, and sesame oil. Pour over chicken and stir-fry 1 to 2 minutes. Serve over hot cooked rice or cool completely, refrigerate, and serve cold.

Hint: Substitute 6 Boneless Chicken Breasts for chicken called for in recipe.

STIR-FRY CHICKEN WITH CASHEWS
4 to 6 servings

2 tablespoons soy sauce
1/2 cup dry sherry or dry white wine
2 tablespoons cornstarch
hot pepper sauce to taste
4 Holly Farms Chicken Breast Halves, 4 Boneless Chicken Breasts, or 6 to 8 Boneless Chicken Thigh Fillets
4 tablespoons peanut oil, divided
1 cup (4 ounces) cashews

1 bunch scallions, cut into 2-inch pieces (green tops included)
1/2 pound mushrooms, sliced
1 small red pepper, seeded and cut into thin strips
1 package (6 ounces) frozen pea pods, thawed
3/4 cup homemade chicken stock (page 24) or canned chicken broth
hot cooked rice to serve

Combine soy sauce, sherry, cornstarch, and hot pepper sauce, stirring until cornstarch is dissolved. Set aside. Remove skin and bones from chicken. Place chicken breasts, 1 at a time, between 2 sheets of plastic wrap and pound with meat mallet or rolling pin to flatten. Cut breasts into chunks and place in glass or china bowl. Pour soy sauce mixture over chicken and toss until well coated. Let stand 15 minutes at room temperature. Drain chicken, reserving marinade. Heat 1 tablespoon peanut oil in wok or large skillet. Add cashews and stir-fry over high heat 1 minute or until lightly toasted. Remove cashews from pan and set aside. Add remaining 3 tablespoons oil to pan. Add chicken and stir-fry 3 minutes or until golden brown. Add scallions, mushrooms, red pepper, and pea pods, and stir well. Add chicken stock, bring to a boil, cover, and simmer 3 to 5 minutes or until vegetables are just crisp. Add reserved soy marinade and cook, stirring constantly, until sauce is thickened. Sprinkle with reserved cashews. Serve immediately over hot cooked rice.

CHICKEN KIEV

6 servings

1/2 cup butter, softened
(no substitute)
2 tablespoons freshly
chopped parsley
1 tablespoon snipped
chives
1 clove garlic, minced
6 Holly Farms Boneless
Chicken Breast Halves
3 tablespoons all-purpose
flour

salt and freshly ground
pepper to taste
1 egg beaten with 1
tablespoon water
about 3/4 cup fine dry
bread crumbs (plain or
seasoned)
vegetable oil for
frying
parsley sprigs for
garnish

Combine butter, parsley, chives, and garlic, and stir until well blended. Place butter mixture on small sheet of plastic wrap. Shape butter into 3-inch square. Wrap and freeze until needed. Place each breast between 2 sheets of plastic wrap and pound with meat mallet or rolling pin to 1/4 inch thickness (take care not to tear chicken). Cut frozen butter mixture into 6 pieces, each 1/2 inch thick. Place 1 piece butter in center of 1 chicken breast. Fold sides over and roll up, enclosing butter completely. Secure end with wooden toothpick if desired. Repeat with remaining butter and chicken breasts. Place flour, salt, and pepper in shallow dish and mix well. Dredge stuffed chicken rolls in flour, dip in beaten egg, shaking off excess, and roll in bread crumbs to coat completely. Place coated chicken rolls on plate or small cookie sheet, cover with waxed paper or plastsic wrap, and refrigerate at least 1 hour. Heat 2 to 3 inches oil in deep-fat fryer or large saucepan. Carefully lower 2 or 3 stuffed breasts into hot oil and deep-fry 12 to 15 minutes or until rolls are deep golden brown and firm. (Do not pierce rolls to test for doneness.) Remove rolls with tongs and drain on paper towels. Deep-fry remaining rolls. To serve, remove and discard toothpicks, arrange rolls on warm serving platter, and garnish with parsley sprigs.

Microwave Method: Prepare and stuff chicken breasts as directed above. Omit dry bread crumbs and substitute 1 1/2 cups toasted fresh bread crumbs. Arrange rolls in circular fashion in greased shallow microproof baking dish. Cover with paper towel and microcook at 100% power 9 to 10 minutes. Serve as directed above.

HUNGARIAN CHICKEN PAPRIKA   *4 servings*

4 Holly Farms Prime
    Chicken Breast Quarters
salt, freshly ground
    pepper, and paprika
    to taste
3 tablespoons vegetable
    oil
1 large onion, chopped
2 large cloves garlic,
    crushed
2 tablespoons paprika

2 tablespoons all-purpose
    flour
1/2 cup homemade chicken
    stock (page 24) or
    canned chicken broth
1 can (16 ounces) crushed
    tomatoes
1/4 cup dry vermouth
1/2 cup dairy sour cream
    freshly chopped parsley
    for garnish (optional)

Tuck wing tips under upper part of wings to flatten. Season chicken with salt, pepper, and paprika. Heat oil in large skillet, add chicken, and brown on both sides. Remove chicken with tongs and set aside. Add onion and garlic to skillet and sauté until onion is transparent. Stir in paprika and flour and cook 1 minute over low heat, stirring constantly. Add stock slowly, stirring. Add tomatoes and vermouth, stir well, and bring to a boil. Return reserved chicken to skillet, spooning tomato mixture over. Lower heat, cover, and simmer 30 to 35 minutes or until chicken is tender, turning chicken occasionally. Remove chicken to deep serving dish. Stir sour cream into sauce, adjust seasoning, and cook over low heat just until heated through. (Do not allow sauce to boil or sour cream will curdle.) Spoon sauce over chicken and sprinkle with parsley. Serve with hot cooked noodles, spaetzle, or mashed potatoes.

Microwave Method: Brown chicken and prepare sauce as directed above, reducing stock to 1/4 cup. Arrange chicken in single layer in microproof baking dish, placing thickest part of chicken at outer edge of dish. Pour tomato mixture over chicken. Cover loosely with plastic wrap and microcook at 100% power 9 minutes. Turn chicken over, recover, and microcook at 100% power 9 to 10 minutes or until tender. Remove chicken to warm serving platter. Stir sour cream into sauce, adjust seasoning, and microcook at 70% power 1 minute or until sauce is just heated through. Serve as directed above.

MOROCCAN CHICKEN
4 servings

1 package Holly Farms
  Whole Chicken Quartered
1 large red onion, thinly
  sliced
3/4 cup olive oil
1 teaspoon ground ginger
1 teaspoon ground
  coriander
1 teaspoon ground cumin
1 teaspoon turmeric
1/4 cup freshly chopped
  parsley

salt and freshly ground
  pepper to taste
1 cup homemade chicken
  stock (page 24) or
  canned chicken broth
4 medium-size potatoes,
  peeled and cut into
  chunks
1 can (16 ounces) whole
  peeled tomatoes,
  drained

Place chicken in single layer in shallow baking dish. Scatter onion slices over chicken. Blend olive oil, ginger, coriander, cumin, turmeric, parsley, salt, and pepper in small bowl, stirring with fork or wire whisk. Pour marinade over chicken, turning to coat. Cover with plastic wrap and refrigerate overnight. Drain marinade from chicken, reserving marinade and onion. Heat 1/4 cup reserved marinade in large skillet. Add chicken and brown well on all sides. Add reserved onion, stock, and remaining marinade. Cover and simmer 25 minutes. Add potatoes and tomatoes to skillet, breaking up tomatoes with back of spoon. Cover and simmer 20 to 25 minutes or until potatoes and chicken are tender. Arrange chicken on serving platter, surround with potatoes, and pour sauce over. Serve hot.

CHA-CHA CHICKEN
4 servings

2 tablespoons olive oil
2 cloves garlic, minced
1 can (16 ounces) crushed
  tomatoes
1 tablespoon chili powder
1 can (4 ounces) chopped
  green chilies, drained
1/2 teaspoon oregano
  salt, freshly ground
  pepper, and cayenne
  to taste

1 package Holly Farms
  Whole Chicken
  Quartered or Split
  Chicken
2 tablespoons vegetable
  oil

Heat olive oil in saucepan, add garlic, and sauté until just golden. Add tomatoes, chili powder, green chilies, oregano, salt, pepper, and cayenne, and stir well. Slowly bring to a boil. Cover, lower heat, and simmer 20 minutes. Remove from heat and set aside. Preheat oven to 375°F. Season chicken with salt and pepper. Lightly brush chicken with vegetable oil. Place chicken, skin side up, in single layer in shallow baking dish. Bake 20 minutes. Remove chicken from oven. Spoon chili-tomato sauce over chicken, covering chicken completely. Return chicken to oven and bake 20 to 25 minutes or until tender, basting chicken occasionally with chili sauce. Arrange chicken on serving platter and spoon sauce over.

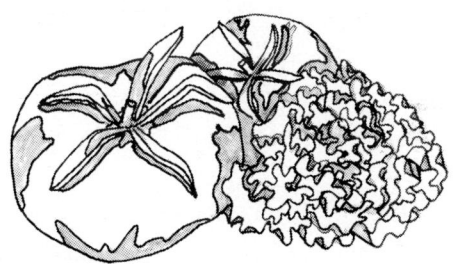

CHICKEN TACOS

6 servings

2 tablespoons butter or margarine
1 medium-size onion, minced
1 clove garlic, minced
2 cups finely shredded cooked chicken (page 93)

1 cup prepared taco sauce (hot preferred)
salt and freshly ground pepper to taste
12 taco shells

Accompaniments:

shredded lettuce
diced tomatoes
avocado slices or guacamole

shredded Cheddar cheese
dairy sour cream
prepared taco, jalapeno, chili, or salsa sauce

Preheat oven to 350°F. Melt butter in skillet. Add onion and garlic and sauté until onion is transparent. Add chicken, 1 cup taco sauce, salt, and pepper, and stir well. Simmer 10 to 12 minutes or until most of liquid has evaporated, stirring occasionally. Remove skillet from heat. Place taco shells on large cookie sheet. Heat in oven 5 to 7 minutes to crisp. Spoon chicken mixture into taco shells. Top with selected accompaniments or arrange filled tacos on large serving platter and surround with bowls of accompaniments.

ARROZ con POLLO

4 to 6 servings

1 package Holly Farms
  Pick of the Chix or
  Country Style Whole
  Chicken Cut Up
  salt and freshly ground
  pepper to taste
1/4 cup olive oil
1 large clove garlic,
  minced
1 large onion, coarsely
  chopped
1 green or red pepper,
  seeded and chopped
2 1/2 cups homemade chicken
  stock (page 24) or
  canned chicken broth

1 can (16 ounces) whole
  peeled tomatoes,
  undrained
1 teaspoon paprika
1/2 teaspoon ground cumin
1/4 teaspoon ground saffron
  or a few saffron
  threads
1 cup rice
1 package (10 ounces)
  frozen tiny peas or
  artichoke hearts, or
  1 can (16 ounces)
  garbanzo beans,
  drained
  pimiento for garnish

Season chicken with salt and pepper. Heat oil in large skillet, add chicken, and brown well on all sides. Remove chicken with tongs and set aside. Preheat oven to 375°F. Add garlic, onion, and green pepper to skillet and sauté until onion is transparent. Add stock, tomatoes, paprika, cumin, saffron, salt, and pepper. Break up tomatoes with back of spoon, add rice, and stir well. Cover and bring to a boil. Transfer to deep 3 1/2-quart casserole. Arrange chicken on top. Cover and bake 35 to 40 minutes or until chicken is tender and all liquid has been absorbed. Cook peas according to package directions and drain well. Fluff rice with fork and add peas. Cut pimiento into strips or decorative shapes. Arrange on top of casserole and bake 5 to 10 minutes. Serve hot.

Arroz con Pollo

SPANISH CHICKEN STEW

4 to 6 servings

3 tablespoons vegetable oil
1 package Holly Farms Country Style Whole Chicken Cut Up
2 cloves garlic, minced
1 large onion, chopped
1 can (28 ounces) whole peeled tomatoes, chopped
1 cup homemade chicken stock (page 24) or canned chicken broth

1 teaspoon thyme
salt and freshly ground pepper to taste
2 medium-size sweet red peppers, seeded and cut into strips
1/2 pound chorizo or linguica sausage, cut into thick slices

Heat oil in Dutch oven, add chicken, and brown on all sides. Remove chicken with slotted spoon and set aside. Add garlic and onion to pan and sauté until onion is transparent. Add tomatoes and their juice, stock, thyme, salt, and pepper, and stir well. Bring to a boil, add reserved chicken, cover, and lower heat. Simmer 40 minutes. Add red pepper strips and chorizo, and simmer, uncovered, 15 minutes or until chicken is tender and peppers are cooked. Serve over hot cooked rice.

Microwave Method: Brown chicken and prepare sauce as directed above, decreasing stock to 2/3 cup. Arrange chicken in single layer in shallow microproof baking dish, placing thickest part of chicken at outer edge of dish. Pour sauce over chicken. Cover loosely and microcook at 100% power 14 minutes, stirring once. Add red peppers and sausage, recover, and microcook at 100% power 6 to 10 minutes or until chicken is tender and peppers are cooked. Serve as directed above.

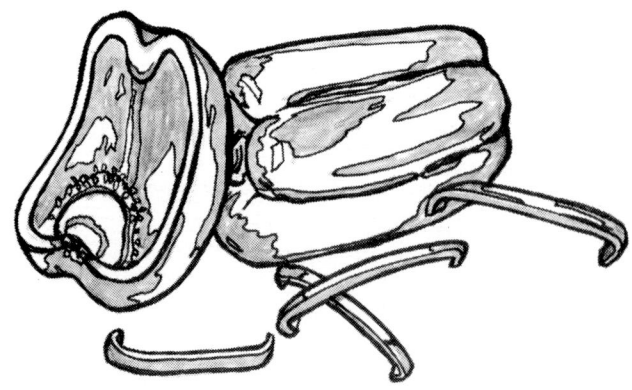

TURKISH THIGHS

4 servings

6 to 8 Holly Farms
   Boneless Chicken Thigh
   Fillets
   salt and freshly ground
   pepper to taste
1/4 cup minced onion
2 tablespoons freshly
   chopped parsley
1/2 teaspoon ground cumin
1/4 teaspoon cinnamon
1/4 teaspoon nutmeg
1/4 teaspoon ground
   coriander
   pinch ground cloves
8 dried apricots

8 whole pitted dates or
   prunes
2 tablespoons melted
   butter, margarine, or
   vegetable oil
   paprika
1/2 cup apricot preserves
1 teaspoon lemon juice
1/2 cup plain yogurt
2 to 3 tablespoons Dijon-
   style mustard
   hot cooked rice to
   serve
   toasted sliced almonds
   for garnish

Place each thigh fillet between 2 sheets of plastic wrap and pound with meat mallet or rolling pin to 1/4-inch thickness. Season thigh fillets with salt and pepper. Preheat oven to 375°F. Combine onion, parsley, cumin, cinnamon, nutmeg, coriander, and cloves in small bowl, and stir until well mixed. Spoon a little onion mixture onto center of each thigh. Place 1 apricot and 1 date in center of each thigh. Fold sides of thighs over fruit stuffing. Place, seam side down, in single layer in shallow baking dish. Brush with melted butter and sprinkle with paprika. Bake 30 to 35 minutes or until chicken is tender, basting occasionally with pan juices. Place preserves and lemon juice in small saucepan over low heat. Cook, stirring, just until preserves are melted. Add yogurt and mustard, stir well, and cook until sauce is heated through. To serve, arrange thighs on bed of rice, spoon sauce over, and sprinkle with almonds. Pour remaining sauce into gravy boat and pass separately.

Microwave Method: Prepare and stuff thighs as directed above. Arrange thighs, seam side down, in circular fashion in 9-inch round microproof dish. Brush with melted butter and sprinkle with paprika. Cover loosely with plastic wrap. Micro-cook at 70% power 7 minutes. Baste with pan juices. Recover and microcook at 50% power 12 to 14 minutes or until chicken is tender. Remove and let stand, covered, until ready to serve. Place preserves, lemon juice, yogurt, and mustard in 2-cup glass measure and stir well. Microcook at 100% power 2 to 3 minutes or until sauce is heated through, stirring after 1 minute. Serve as directed above.

APRICOT-GINGER CHICKEN
6 servings

1 tablespoon melted butter
  or margarine
1 package Holly Farms
  Pick of the Chix
1 can (16 ounces) apricot
  halves, undrained
1 large clove garlic,
  minced
1 tablespoon fresh minced
  gingerroot, or 1 teaspoon
  ground ginger

2 tablespoons cider
  vinegar or malt
  vinegar
2 tablespoons light soy
  sauce
salt and freshly ground
  pepper to taste
toasted sliced or
  slivered almonds for
  garnish

Place wire rack over roasting pan and brush rack with melted butter. Arrange chicken on wire rack and set aside. Place apricots, garlic, gingerroot, vinegar, and soy sauce in container of blender or food processor and process to coarse purée. Pour apricot purée into saucepan, season with salt and pepper, and bring to a boil. Boil rapidly 2 to 3 minutes, stirring constantly, until sauce is thickened and coats back of spoon. Remove from heat. Preheat oven to 375°F. Brush chicken liberally on all sides with apricot sauce, reserving some sauce for basting. Bake 35 to 40 minutes or until chicken is tender, turning once or twice and brushing with reserved sauce. Arrange chicken on warm serving platter and sprinkle with almonds just before serving.

Variation: If desired, skin may be removed from chicken because sauce will keep chicken moist.

FRUITY CHICKEN PARCELS
4 servings

1 tablespoon butter or
  margarine
1 tablespoon vegetable oil
4 Holly Farms Prime
  Chicken Legs
4 tablespoons honey
4 tablespoons raisins

4 teaspoons freshly grated
  gingerroot or 1 teaspoon
  ground ginger
4 teaspoons sliced or
  slivered almonds
salt and freshly ground
  pepper to taste

Cut 4 pieces of aluminum foil, each large enough to wrap around 1 chicken leg. Set aside. Melt butter and oil in skillet. Add chicken and cook over high heat until browned on all sides. Place 1 chicken leg in center of each piece of foil. Spoon 1 tablespoon honey and 1 tablespoon raisins over each chicken leg. Sprinkle each with 1 teaspoon grated gingerroot (or 1/4 teaspoon ground ginger) and 1 teaspoon almonds. Season with salt and pepper. Preheat oven to 375°F. Bring sides of foil together and seal edges to completely enclose each chicken leg. Place parcels on cookie sheet in single layer and bake 1 hour or until chicken is tender. Serve chicken in parcels accompanied by hot cooked noodles and a fresh vegetable.

CHICKEN CURRY WITH ACCOMPANIMENTS

4 servings

1 package Holly Farms Whole Chicken Quartered
salt, freshly ground pepper, and paprika to taste
4 tablespoons vegetable oil
2 onions, chopped
3 cloves garlic, minced
2 tablespoons all-purpose flour
2 tablespoons curry powder
1 tablespoon freshly minced gingerroot or 1 teaspoon ground ginger

1/8 teaspoon cayenne
1 1/2 cups homemade chicken stock (page 24) or canned chicken broth
1 tablespoon lemon juice
1 large tomato, peeled, seeded, and diced
1 cup coconut milk or plain yogurt
hot cooked rice to serve

Accompaniments:

toasted shredded coconut
peach or mango chutney
diced cucumber mixed with sliced scallions

raisins mixed with slivered almonds
salted peanuts

Season chicken with salt, pepper, and paprika. Heat oil in large skillet. Add chicken and brown well on all sides. Remove chicken with tongs and set aside. Add onions and garlic to skillet and sauté until onions are transparent. Stir in flour, curry powder, gingerroot, and cayenne, and cook 2 minutes, stirring. Add lemon juice, stock, and tomato, and cook, stirring, until sauce is thickened and comes to a boil. Return chicken to skillet, lower heat, cover, and simmer 30 to 35 minutes or until chicken is tender. Remove chicken to warm serving platter. Skim fat from sauce in skillet, bring sauce to a boil, and boil rapidly 3 minutes to reduce. Lower heat, stir in coconut milk, and cook just until heated through. Spoon sauce over chicken and serve with hot cooked rice and an assortment of accompaniments in small bowls.

GLAZED THIGHS
6 servings

12 Holly Farms Prime
    Chicken Thighs or 6
    Thighs and 6 Drumsticks
salt and freshly ground
    pepper to taste

vegetable oil
glaze (see below)

Season chicken with salt and pepper and brush lightly with oil. Place thighs, skin side down, on rack in broiler pan. Broil 4 to 6 inches from source of heat 20 minutes. Turn thighs over and broil 10 minutes. Turn thighs again and brush liberally with glaze. Broil 5 minutes or until chicken is tender, turning and brushing with glaze. Serve immediately.

Curry Fruit Glaze:

1 cup peach, pineapple, or
    apricot preserves
1 tablespoon curry powder

3 tablespoons orange
    juice or water

Combine preserves, curry powder, and juice until well blended. Brush over chicken.

Microwave Method: Arrange chicken, skin side down, in single layer in shallow microproof baking dish, placing thickest part of chicken at outer edge of dish. Brush with glaze (see above), cover loosely, and microcook at 100% power 10 minutes. Turn chicken over, brush with glaze, recover, and microcook at 100% power 8 to 10 minutes or until chicken is tender. Let stand 5 minutes.

Ruby Glaze:

2/3 cup red currant jelly
2 tablespoons Dijon-style
    or spicy brown mustard

1/4 teaspoon ground cloves

Place jelly in small saucepan over low heat and cook, stirring constantly, just until jelly is melted. Let cool slightly. Add mustard and cloves and stir until well blended. Brush over chicken.

Ruby Glaze Microwave Method: Place jelly in 2-cup glass measure. Cover and microcook at 100% power 1 1/2 to 2 minutes or until melted. Add mustard and cloves and stir well.

Glazed Thighs, Sherried Broiled Legs (page 74)

Piquant Glaze:

1/2 cup ketchup	1 1/2 teaspoons dry mustard
1/3 cup firmly packed	1 teaspoon nutmeg
brown sugar	

Combine ketchup, brown sugar, mustard, and nutmeg until well blended. Brush over chicken.

Honey Orange Glaze:

1/2 cup orange marmalade	1 to 2 tablespoons steak
1/2 cup honey	sauce

Mash marmalade with fork. Add honey and steak sauce and stir until well blended. Brush over chicken.

Variation: Omit marmalade. Use 1/3 cup frozen concentrated orange juice, thawed. Add 1 to 2 tablespoons grated orange rind if desired.

SHERRIED BROILED LEGS   *4 servings*

4 Holly Farms Prime	1 egg yolk, beaten
Chicken Legs	1/3 cup thinly sliced
1/3 cup soy sauce	scallions
1/3 cup dry sherry	1/4 teaspoon cayenne
1 tablespoon super fine	scallion tassels for
sugar	garnish
4 teaspoons all-purpose	
flour	

Place chicken in single layer in shallow glass baking dish. Combine soy sauce, sherry, and sugar, and stir until well blended. Pour marinade over chicken, turning chicken to coat evenly. Cover and refrigerate 8 hours or overnight, turning chicken occasionally. Cover broiler rack with aluminum foil. Remove chicken from marinade, reserving marinade. Broil chicken 4 to 6 inches from source of heat 12 minutes on each side. Blend flour with reserved marinade until smooth. Add beaten egg yolk, scallions, and cayenne, and stir until well mixed. Brush chicken generously with mixture and broil 10 to 12 minutes or until chicken is cooked through, turning and brushing chicken with sauce at least 4 times. Arrange chicken on warm serving platter, garnish with scallion tassels, and serve on a bed of cooked vermicelli.

CHICKEN BREASTS DIJON

4 servings

2 Holly Farms Whole
   Chicken Breasts or
   4 Breast Halves
   cracked or freshly
   ground pepper to taste
4 tablespoons Dijon-style
   mustard
3 tablespoons vegetable
   oil
2 tablespoons tarragon
   vinegar or dry white
   wine

1 tablespoon freshly
   chopped tarragon or
   1 teaspoon dried
   tarragon
hot cooked rice or
   noodles to serve
cherry tomatoes for
   garnish

Preheat oven to 350°F. Season chicken with pepper. Place, skin side down, in single layer in shallow baking pan. Blend mustard, oil, vinegar, and tarragon until well mixed. Liberally brush chicken with mustard mixture. Bake 20 minutes. Turn chicken over, brush with mustard mixture, and bake 20 to 25 minutes or until chicken is tender, brushing with mustard mixture several times. Arrange chicken breasts on bed of hot cooked rice or noodles. Garnish with cherry tomatoes.

Variation: Omit tarragon and use 1 tablespoon freshly chopped dill or 1 teaspoon dried dill. Proceed as directed above.

Microwave Method: Season chicken with pepper and place in single layer, skin side down, in shallow microproof baking dish, placing thickest part of breasts toward the outer edge of dish. Blend mustard, oil, vinegar and tarragon, and liberally brush over chicken. Cover loosely and microcook at 100% power 8 minutes. Turn chicken over, brush with mustard mixture, recover, and microcook at 100% power 8 to 10 minutes or until chicken is tender. Serve as directed above.

GARLIC LOVER'S CHICKEN
6 servings

6 **Holly Farms Prime Chicken Legs or Prime Chicken Leg Quarters**
salt and freshly ground pepper to taste
3 **tablespoons olive oil, divided**
2 **tablespoons butter**
40 **whole cloves garlic, peeled (about 3 to 4 garlic bulbs)**
2 **stalks celery, sliced**
2 **leeks, sliced (white part only)**
1/2 **cup homemade chicken stock (page 24) or canned chicken broth**
1/2 **cup dry white wine or dry vermouth**
3 **sprigs parsley**
1 **bay leaf**

Preheat oven to 350°F. Season chicken with salt and pepper. Heat 2 tablespoons olive oil and butter in large flameproof casserole with tight fitting lid. Add chicken and brown well on all sides. Remove chicken with tongs and set aside. Add remaining 1 tablespoon oil, garlic cloves, celery, and leeks to casserole, and stir well. Sauté 3 minutes (do not let garlic brown). Return chicken to casserole. Add stock, wine, parsley, and bay leaf, and bring to a boil. Remove from heat, cover casserole tightly with aluminum foil, and place lid on top of foil. Bake 1 hour 30 minutes. Do not uncover during baking. Place chicken on warm serving platter. Skim fat from liquid in casserole. Remove and discard bay leaf and parsley. Mash garlic in casserole with back of spoon and stir with liquid to mix well. Pour over chicken or pour into gravy boat and serve separately.

LEMON-TARRAGON BROILER
4 servings

1 **package Holly Farms Split Chicken or Whole Chicken Quartered**
paprika
1/4 **cup vegetable or olive oil**
1/4 **cup lemon juice**
1 **tablespoon grated lemon zest (optional)**
1 **teaspoon tarragon**
1 **teaspoon salt**
1/4 **teaspoon pepper**
lemon wedges and sprigs of tarragon or parsley for garnish

Season chicken lightly with paprika. Place chicken, skin side down, on rack in broiler pan. Blend oil, lemon juice, zest, tarragon, salt, and pepper until thoroughly mixed and brush over chicken. Broil chicken 4 to 6 inches from source of heat 20 minutes, brushing occasionally with basting sauce. Turn chicken over and brush with sauce. Broil 20 to 25 minutes or until chicken is tender and nicely browned, brushing occasionally with sauce. Arrange chicken on serving platter and garnish with lemon wedges and sprigs of tarragon.

CHICKEN IN RED WINE   *4 to 6 servings*

1 tablespoon vegetable oil	1 cup dry red wine
1/4 cup diced salt pork	1/2 cup homemade chicken
1 package Holly Farms	stock (page 24) or
Pick of the Chix	canned chicken broth
1/2 pound pearl onions	1/2 teaspoon thyme
2 cloves garlic, minced	salt and freshly ground
1 pound mushrooms, sliced	pepper to taste
2 tablespoons all-purpose flour	

Heat oil in large skillet, add salt pork, and cook until browned and crisp. Remove salt pork with slotted spoon and discard. Add chicken to skillet and brown on all sides. Remove chicken with tongs and set aside. Add onions, garlic, and mushrooms to skillet and sauté 3 to 4 minutes or until onions are lightly browned. Sprinkle flour over onion-mushroom mixture and cook, stirring, 1 minute. Add wine, stock, thyme, salt, and pepper, and bring to a boil. Return chicken to skillet, lower heat, cover, and simmer 30 to 35 minutes or until chicken is tender. Arrange chicken, mushrooms, and onions on warm serving platter. Boil sauce in pan 2 to 3 minutes to reduce. Pour sauce over chicken or serve separately.

Microwave Method: Brown chicken and prepare sauce as directed above, reducing wine to 3/4 cup. Arrange chicken pieces in 2 1/2-quart microproof baking dish in single layer, placing thickest part of chicken at outer edge of dish. Pour sauce mixture over chicken. Cover loosely and microcook at 100% power 15 to 18 minutes or until chicken is tender, stirring once. Let stand 5 minutes. Serve as directed above.

WINTER CHICKEN AND POTATO CASSEROLE

8 servings

1 cup all-purpose flour
    salt and freshly ground
    pepper to taste
2 packages Holly Farms
    Pick of the Chix or
    Country Style Whole
    Chicken Cut Up
6 tablespoons vegetable
    oil
2 onions, chopped
1 pound mushrooms, sliced
4 cups homemade chicken
    stock (page 24) or
    canned chicken broth

1 teaspoon thyme
3 tablespoons freshly
    chopped parsley
8 to 12 new potatoes,
    peeled
1 pound baby carrots
1 cup coarsely chopped
    celery
6 slices bacon, cooked
    and crumbled

Place flour in plastic bag and season with salt and pepper. Add 2 chicken pieces and shake bag vigorously until chicken is well coated. Set coated chicken aside and repeat with remaining chicken. Reserve excess flour. Heat oil in large skillet, add chicken pieces, and cook until browned on all sides. Remove chicken with tongs and set aside. Add onion and mushrooms to skillet and sauté until onion is transparent. Sprinkle reserved seasoned flour over onion-mushroom mixture and cook, stirring, 1 minute. Gradually stir in stock and cook, sitrring, until mixture comes to a boil and thickens. Add thyme, parsley, salt, and pepper. Stir well and set aside. Preheat oven to 375°F. Place chicken, potatoes, carrots, and celery in casserole. Season with salt and pepper. Pour reserved sauce over. Cover and bake 1 hour to 1 hour 15 minutes or until chicken is tender and vegetables are cooked. Sprinkle with bacon and serve directly from casserole.

Winter Chicken and Potato Casserole

BOSTON DRUMSTICK AND BEAN CASSEROLE

3 to 4 servings

3 tablespoons vegetable oil
6 Holly Farms Prime Chicken Drumsticks
1 can (28 ounces) brick oven baked beans
1 large onion, chopped
1 large green or red pepper, seeded and chopped
1 can (8 ounces) tomato sauce
1/4 cup molasses
1 teaspoon dry mustard
salt and freshly ground pepper to taste
4 slices bacon, cooked and crumbled

Heat oil in skillet and brown drumsticks on all sides. Place drumsticks in deep 2 1/2-quart casserole. Preheat oven to 350°F. Combine beans, onion, green pepper, tomato sauce, molasses, mustard, salt, and pepper in bowl, and stir until well mixed. Spoon over drumsticks. Cover and bake 1 hour, stirring occasionally. Uncover and scatter bacon over casserole. Bake 15 minutes or until drumsticks are tender. Serve with warm brown bread for a hearty meal.

Microwave Method: Brown drumsticks as directed above. Combine beans, onion, green pepper, tomato sauce, molasses, mustard, salt, and pepper in 2 1/2 to 3-quart microproof casserole. Stir until well blended. Add drumsticks, pushing them down into the beans. Cover loosely and microcook at 100% power 12 to 16 minutes or until drumsticks are tender, stirring after 8 minutes and pushing drumsticks back down into beans. Serve as directed above.

LOUISIANA CHICKEN CASSEROLE

4 to 6 servings

1 package Holly Farms Country Style Whole Chicken Cut Up
2 cups chopped onions, divided
salt and freshly ground pepper to taste
1 jar (8 1/4 ounces) dry roasted unsalted peanuts
4 tablespoons peanut oil, divided
1 pound okra, trimmed and sliced
2 to 3 fresh green chilies, seeded and finely chopped
1 cup chopped tomato
1 tablespoon tomato paste

Place chicken, 1 cup onions, salt, and pepper in large saucepan. Pour in enough cold water to cover and bring to a boil. Lower heat, cover, and cook 25 to 30 minutes or until chicken is just tender, skimming surface of water as necessary. Remove chicken with slotted spoon and set aside to cool. Strain cooking liquid, reserving 2 1/2 cups. Place peanuts in container of blender or food processor and process to coarse paste (do not overprocess). Set aside. Heat 1 tablespoon oil in large saucepan, add okra, and sauté 5 minutes, turning occasionally. Remove okra with slotted spoon and set aside. Heat remaining 3 tablespoons oil in same saucepan, add remaining 1 cup onions and chilies, and sauté 5 minutes or until onion is transparent. Remove pan from heat and add reserved peanut paste. Gradually stir in reserved 2 1/2 cups cooking liquid until well blended. Add tomato and tomato paste, and stir until thoroughly combined. Remove and discard skin from chicken and place chicken in deep casserole. Pour peanut-tomato mixture over chicken, turning to coat chicken evenly. Cover and let stand at room temperature about 1 hour to blend flavors. Preheat oven to 350°F. Add reserved okra to chicken, stir gently, cover, and bake 20 to 30 minutes or until heated through. Adjust seasoning and serve immediately.

RICE AND WING CASSEROLE   6 servings

16 to 18 Holly Farms Prime Chicken Wings
salt and freshly ground pepper to taste
2 tablespoons butter or margarine
1 1/2 cups chopped onions
3 cloves garlic, minced
1 1/2 cups rice
3 1/2 cups homemade chicken stock (page 24) or canned chicken broth
1 cup fresh or canned chopped tomatoes
1 teaspoon oregano
hot pepper sauce to taste
1 red or green pepper, seeded and chopped
1 cup frozen peas, thawed
1 cup diced zucchini or frozen cut green beans, thawed

Fold wing tips under upper part of wings and season with salt and pepper. Melt butter in deep 4-quart flameproof casserole. Add wings and brown well on both sides. Remove wings from casserole and set aside. Preheat oven to 375°F. Add onions and garlic to casserole and sauté until onions are transparent. Add rice and stir to coat. Return chicken wings to casserole. Add stock, tomatoes, oregano, salt, pepper, and hot pepper sauce. Stir well and bring to a boil. Cover and bake 15 minutes. Add red pepper, peas, and zucchini, and mix well. Recover and bake 10 minutes or until all liquid has been absorbed and chicken is tender. Spoon onto large serving platter.

BRUNSWICK STEW

6 *servings*

1 package Holly Farms
Three Legged Chicken or
Whole Chicken Cut Up
salt and freshly ground
pepper to taste
1/4 cup vegetable oil
1 large onion, chopped
2 stalks celery, cut into
chunks
1/2 cup chopped green pepper
4 cups homemade chicken
stock (page 24) or
canned chicken broth
1 can (16 ounces) whole
peeled tomatoes or
stewed tomatoes

1 tablespoon Worcester-
shire sauce
1/4 teaspoon cayenne or to
taste
1 bay leaf
1 package (10 ounces)
frozen baby lima beans
1 package (10 ounces)
frozen whole kernel
corn
1/4 cup all-purpose flour

Split breast in half and season chicken with salt and pepper. Heat oil in large Dutch oven. Add chicken and brown well on all sides. Remove chicken with tongs and set aside. Add onion, celery, and green pepper to pan, and sauté until onion is transparent. Add stock, tomatoes, Worcestershire, cayenne, bay leaf, salt, and pepper. Break up tomatoes with back of spoon and bring to a boil. Return chicken to pan, lower heat, cover, and simmer 30 minutes. Add lima beans and corn and simmer 20 minutes. Remove and discard bay leaf. Blend flour with 1/2 cup water until smooth. Slowly stir into stew. Cook, stirring, until thickened. Simmer 5 minutes and serve immediately.

Microwave Method: Brown chicken in skillet as directed above and arrange in 4-quart microproof casserole, placing thickest part of chicken at outer edge of dish. Combine onion, celery, green pepper, 3 cups stock, tomatoes, Worcestershire, cayenne, salt, pepper, and bay leaf in large bowl and stir until well mixed. Pour over chicken. Cover loosely and microcook at 100% power 20 minutes stirring once. Remove and discard bay leaf. Blend flour with 1/2 cup water until smooth and stir into stew. Add lima beans and corn and stir well. Recover and micro-cook at 70% power 18 to 22 minutes, or until chicken is tender and vegetables are cooked, stirring twice during cooking.

Brunswick Stew

COUNTRY CAPTAIN
6 servings

1/2 cup all-purpose flour
1 teaspoon salt
1/2 teaspoon paprika
1/4 teaspoon pepper
6 Holly Farms Prime Chicken Thighs and 6 Prime Chicken Drumsticks or 1 package Best of the Fryer
1/4 cup vegetable oil
2 large cloves garlic, minced
1 cup chopped onions
1 green pepper, seeded and chopped
1/4 cup freshly chopped parsley
1 tablespoon curry powder
1/2 teaspoon thyme
1/2 teaspoon cayenne or to taste
1 1/2 cups homemade chicken stock (page 24) or canned chicken broth
1 can (28 ounces) whole peeled tomatoes, or 1 can (28 ounces) crushed tomatoes
1/2 cup raisins or currants hot cooked rice to serve
1/4 cup toasted sliced almonds for garnish

Place flour, salt, paprika, and pepper in plastic bag. Add 2 chicken pieces and shake bag vigorously until chicken is well coated. Set coated chicken aside and repeat with remaining chicken. Reserve excess flour. Heat oil in Dutch oven. Add chicken and brown well on all sides. Remove chicken with tongs and set aside. Add garlic, onions, and green pepper to pan, and sauté until onions are transparent. Stir in parsley, curry powder, thyme, and cayenne, and cook, stirring, 1 minute. Add stock, tomatoes, and raisins. Break up tomatoes with back of spoon and stir well. Bring to a boil. Return chicken to pan, cover, and lower heat. Simmer 50 to 60 minutes or until chicken is tender. Blend reserved seasoned flour with 1/2 cup cold water and stir into stew. Cook, stirring occasionally, until thickened. Taste and adjust seasoning. Spoon stew over hot cooked rice and sprinkle with almonds. Serve immediately.

LEMON-CHICKEN CAPER
4 servings

4 Holly Farms Boneless Chicken Breasts or 8 Boneless Chicken Thigh Fillets
1/4 cup all-purpose flour salt and freshly ground pepper to taste
1 teaspoon paprika
2 to 3 tablespoons butter or margarine
2 to 3 tablespoons vegetable oil
2/3 cup homemade chicken stock (page 24) or canned chicken broth juice of 1 lemon
2 tablespoons drained capers, chopped freshly chopped parsley for garnish

Cut chicken into 1/4-inch thick strips. Place flour in large plastic bag, add salt, pepper, and paprika, and shake to blend.

Add half the chicken strips to seasoned flour and shake vigorously until chicken strips are well coated. Melt 2 tablespoons butter and 2 tablespoons oil in skillet. Add coated chicken strips and cook over high heat, stirring, until chicken is browned on all sides. Remove with slotted spoon and drain on paper towels. Coat and cook remaining chicken, adding more butter and oil to skillet if necessary. Remove chicken from skillet and drain on paper towels. Add stock and lemon juice to skillet and bring to a boil, scraping up browned particles in skillet. Add reserved chicken strips and capers, and cook 2 to 3 minutes or until chicken is heated through. Place on warm serving dish and sprinkle with parsley. Serve immediately with hot cooked spinach noodles.

CHICKEN HOTPOT

6 servings

1 package Holly Farms Three Legged Chicken or Whole Chicken Cut Up

4 tablespoons vegetable oil

1 large onion, coarsely chopped

2 cups sliced carrots

1 cup diced yellow turnip or parsnip

4 cups homemade chicken stock (page 24) or canned chicken broth

2 tablespoons tomato paste grated Cheddar cheese to serve

1 bouquet garni consisting of: 2 sprigs parsley, 1 clove garlic, 1 bay leaf, 1/2 teaspoon thyme leaves, and a few black peppercorns* salt and freshly ground pepper to taste

4 medium-size potatoes, peeled and cut into chunks

1 bunch leeks, rinsed, trimmed, and thickly sliced

Cut chicken breast in half. Heat oil in Dutch oven, add chicken, and brown on all sides. Remove chicken with tongs and set aside. Add onion and carrots to pan and sauté until onion is transparent. Add turnip, stock, tomato paste, bouquet garni, salt, and pepper. Stir well and bring to a boil. Skim off excess fat and return chicken pieces to pan. Lower heat, cover, and simmer 30 minutes. Add potatoes and leeks and simmer 20 minutes or until chicken is tender and vegetables are cooked. Remove and discard bouquet garni. Ladle into deep bowls and pass cheese separately.

*NOTE: To make a bouquet garni, wrap herbs in small piece of cheesecloth and tie with kitchen string. Ready-made bouquets garnis can be purchased in specialty food stores and in food departments of large department stores.

CHICKEN DUPONT
4 servings

1 package Holly Farms Country Style Whole Chicken Cut Up or Whole Chicken Cut Up
salt and freshly ground pepper to taste
4 tablespoons vegetable oil or shortening
1 onion, thinly sliced
1/2 pound mushrooms, sliced
1 can (16 ounces) stewed tomatoes
1/2 cup homemade chicken stock (page 24) or canned chicken broth
1/2 cup dry vermouth or dry white wine
1 teaspoon basil
4 teaspoons all-purpose flour
1 tablespoon freshly chopped parsley for garnish

Preheat oven to 375°F. Season chicken with salt and pepper. Heat oil in deep flameproof casserole. Add chicken and cook until browned on all sides. Remove chicken with tongs and set aside. Add onion and mushrooms to casserole and sauté until onion is transparent. Add tomatoes, stock, vermouth, and basil. Stir well, breaking up tomatoes with back of spoon. Bring to a boil and remove from heat. Add reserved chicken, cover, and bake 30 minutes. Uncover and bake 20 to 25 minutes or until chicken is tender. Remove chicken to serving platter and keep warm. Stir 2 tablespoons tomato mixture into flour to make smooth paste and add to casserole. Cook over high heat, stirring, until sauce is slightly thickened. Spoon sauce over chicken and sprinkle with parsley.

HERB-CRUMBED CHICKEN BREASTS
4 servings

1/4 cup vegetable or olive oil
1/4 cup dry white wine
1 tablespoon Dijon-style mustard
1 tablespoon lemon juice
3 tablespoons freshly chopped parsley, divided
1 teaspoon basil, divided
1/2 teaspoon oregano
4 Holly Farms Prime Chicken Breast Halves with Ribs
1 1/2 cups fresh bread crumbs
1/2 teaspoon thyme
salt and freshly ground pepper to taste
1 egg, beaten

Combine oil, wine, mustard, lemon juice, 1 tablespoon parsley, 1/2 teaspoon basil, and oregano, and mix to blend. Place chicken in shallow glass baking dish. Pour marinade over chicken, turning to coat. Cover and refrigerate 2 hours, turning occasionally. Preheat oven to 350°F. Remove chicken from refrigerator, uncover, turn skin side up, and bake in marinade 25 to 30 minutes or until almost tender, basting several times during cooking. Mix remaining 2 tablespoons parsley, bread crumbs, remaining 1/2 teaspoon basil, thyme, salt, pepper, and beaten egg. Remove chicken from oven and spread bread crumb mixture on top of each chicken breast, patting mixture down with back of spoon. Baste bread crumb topping with pan juices. Return chicken to oven and bake about 15 minutes or until bread crumb topping is browned and chicken is cooked through. Spoon pan juices over chicken and serve.

CHICKEN AND HAM GUMBO   *6 to 8 servings*

1 Holly Farms Hen, cut into serving pieces
salt and freshly ground pepper to taste
1/2 cup vegetable oil
6 tablespoons all-purpose flour
1 clove garlic, minced
1 large onion, chopped
1 green pepper, seeded and chopped
1/2 pound lean cooked ham, cut into cubes
1/4 cup freshly chopped parsley
2 bay leaves
1/2 teaspoon thyme
1/4 teaspoon cayenne
1 pound okra, trimmed and thickly sliced
1 to 1 1/2 tablespoons file powder (optional)
hot cooked rice

Season chicken with salt and pepper. Heat oil in Dutch oven, add chicken, and brown on all sides. Remove hen with tongs and set aside. Add flour to pan and cook, stirring constantly, until roux is smooth and lightly browned. Add garlic, onion, green pepper, and ham. Cook over low heat 10 minutes, stirring occasionally. Add 8 cups water, parsley, bay leaves, thyme, cayenne, and reserved chicken pieces. Bring to a boil, cover, lower heat, and simmer 1 hour or until chicken is almost tender. Add okra and simmer 20 to 25 minutes, stirring occasionally. Remove from heat and remove and discard bay leaves. Stir in file powder and let stand 5 minutes. Spoon rice into deep soup bowls and ladle gumbo over rice.

CHICKEN KABOBS
4 servings

4 Holly Farms Boneless
   Chicken Breasts
4 to 6 Holly Farms
   Boneless Chicken Thigh
   Fillets
4 small zucchini, trimmed
1/2 cup olive oil
1/4 cup cider vinegar
2 tablespoons lemon juice
1 large onion, minced

1 teaspoon thyme
1 teaspoon basil
1 teaspoon paprika
   salt and freshly ground
   pepper to taste
1 bay leaf
1 large red pepper, seeded
   and cut into 8 chunks
   hot cooked rice to
   serve

Cut each chicken breast into 4 pieces. Cut small thighs in half or large thighs into 4 pieces. Cut each zucchini into 4 chunks, about 1-inch thick. Combine olive oil, vinegar, lemon juice, onion, thyme, basil, paprika, salt, pepper, and bay leaf, and mix well. Place chicken and zucchini chunks in large glass bowl. Pour marinade over and stir gently to coat. Cover and marinate in refrigerator at least 3 hours. Drain and reserve marinade, discarding bay leaf. Thread four 10- or 12-inch metal skewers with red pepper and alternating chicken and zucchini chunks, ending with red pepper. Brush with reserved marinade. Grill over hot coals 20 to 25 minutes or until chicken is tender, brushing several times with reserved marinade and turning at least 2 or 3 times. Serve over a bed of hot cooked rice.

Variation: Add cherry tomatoes to skewers during last 10 minutes of cooking.

Hint: Lightly oil skewers before threading with food. Food will slide on and off oiled skewers easily.

All About Chicken

WHY TAKE A CHANCE WHEN YOU CAN TAKE HOME HOLLY FARMS? THERE IS A DIFFERENCE!

Off To A Great Start With Proper Preparation and Storage

Immediate Use of Chicken:

If you plan to cook chicken the same day you buy it, place the wrapped chicken in the refrigerator as soon as you get home. When you are ready to cook, remove the chicken from the package. Take out the neck and giblets and set them aside. Rinse the chicken under cold running water and pat it dry with paper towels. (If the chicken is to be fried take extra care to be certain the chicken is completely dry in order to prevent hot oil from splattering.)

Separate and set aside any part of the chicken you may not be planning to use immediately. This might include a portion of chicken you want to save and cook for a separate meal, fat that can be rendered (page 98), or backs, necks, or giblets to be used for stock, gravy, or a special recipe. Wrap, label, date, and freeze the portions you do not plan to cook.

Refrigerator Storage:

If you don't intend to use your chicken immediately, but plan to cook it within two days of purchase, store it in the coldest part of the refrigerator in its protective package. The Holly Farms package is specially designed to keep moisture in and airborne bacteria out. Refrigerator temperature should be between 35°F and 40°F. (Incidentally, it is a good idea to invest in an inexpensive refrigerator/freezer thermometer so you can check the temperature of both your refrigerator and freezer regularly.) Don't rinse the chicken until you are ready to cook it.

Freezer Storage:

The Holly Farms package is also designed for use in your freezer. It is not necessary to rewrap an unopened package unless there is a tear in it. However, if you wish, you can rewrap the chicken tightly in freezer wrap or aluminum foil. Be sure to wrap the package tightly and seal well in order to prevent freezer burn. Properly wrapped chicken may be stored safely in the freezer at between 0°F and -10°F for as long as twelve months.

Frozen chicken that has begun to thaw should not be refrozen unless ice crystals are still present. Successive refreezing could adversely affect the quality of the meat.

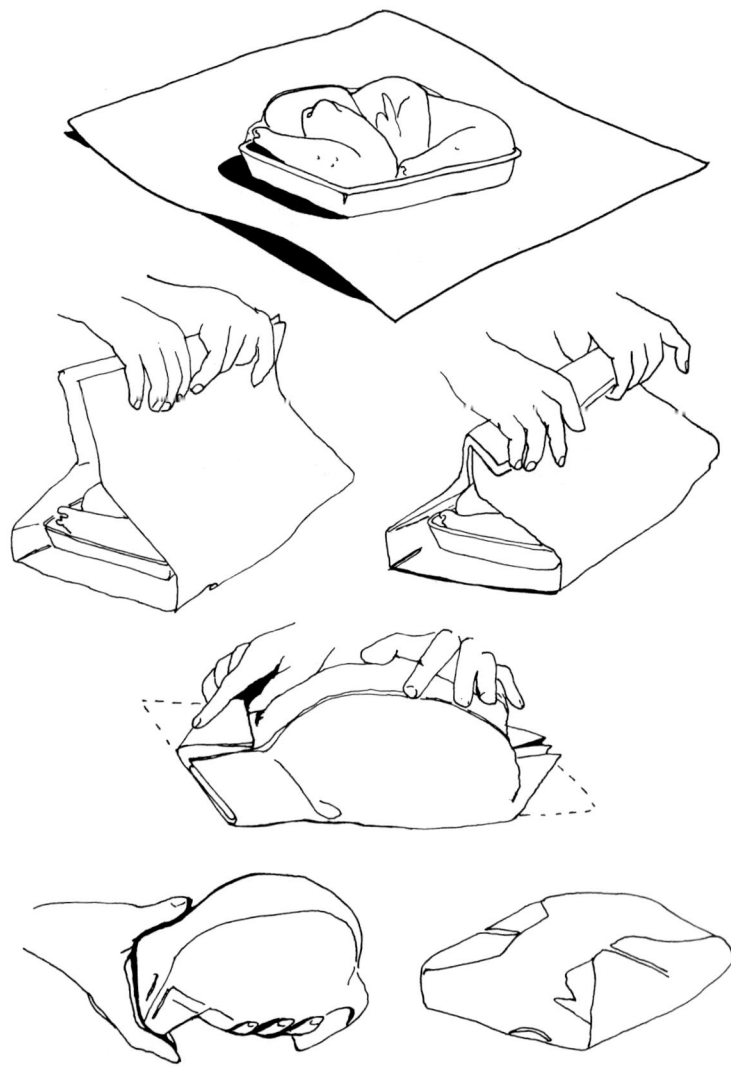

How To Thaw Chicken:

Chicken should be thawed in the refrigerator, still wrapped in the package in which it was frozen. Allow a minimum of sixteen hours to defrost a whole uncut chicken in the refrigerator, and at least six hours to defrost cut chicken or chicken parts. It is a good idea to place frozen chicken on a plate in order to prevent any liquid from dripping onto other food or in the refrigerator as the chicken thaws.

Chicken should not be thawed at room temperature because this will promote bacterial growth, particularly in warm weather. If it is necessary to speed thawing, remove from the refrigerator and place the tightly wrapped chicken in a pan of cold water and change the water occasionally during thawing.

The quickest way to defrost chicken is in a microwave oven. If you have one, follow the manufacturer's instructions for your particular oven. Most microwave thawing is accomplished by placing the packaged chicken on a microproof plate. Remove the metal clamp, if present, from whole chickens. Defrost at 30% power for approximately six minutes per pound, turning the chicken after half the estimated time. Let stand about twenty minutes.

How To Store Leftover Chicken

Refrigerator Storage:

Cool chicken completely. Remove stuffing from roast chicken and place the leftover stuffing in a separate container. Wrap the chicken tightly in plastic wrap or aluminum foil, or place it in a rigid airtight container and store it in the coldest part of the refrigerator. Use the chicken within three or four days; use the stuffing or gravy within two days.

Freezer Storage:

Cool chicken completely. Remove the stuffing from roast chicken and place the leftover stuffing in a rigid airtight container. Wrap the chicken tightly in freezer wrap or aluminum foil, or place it in a rigid airtight container. Label and date the package, and place it in the freezer. Use slices or small pieces of chicken within one month; slices or small pieces of chicken covered with broth within four months; casseroles within four months; and fried chicken within four months.

Frozen cooked chicken should not be refrozen after it has been thawed.

How Much Chicken To Buy?

The correct amount of chicken to buy depends on many factors: number of people to be served; portion size; amount of food to be served with the chicken; ratio of bone to meat in different cuts of chicken; and whether or not you want to plan for leftovers.

When buying a whole chicken you will need:

Roast chicken: 3/4 to 1 pound per person
Broiled or barbecued chicken: about 1 pound (or half a chicken) per person
Stewed chicken: 1/2 to 1 pound per person

When you buy chicken pieces, use the following chart to estimate how much chicken you will get from the different parts of the chicken. In most cases you can figure about six to eight ounces of chicken per person, or about three to four ounces of boneless meat.

Pieces	Weight
Breast half	about 6 ounces
Drumstick	about 3 ounces
Thigh	about 4 ounces
Quartered Chicken	
Breast quarter	about 11 ounces
Leg quarter	about 11 ounces

Estimating amount of uncooked chicken needed for cups of cooked chicken.

Many recipes throughout this book call for cooked chicken that is cubed, diced, ground, or slivered. When the amount of cooked chicken called for in a recipe is small, these recipes provide wonderful ways to use leftover chicken. But there are sure to be times when you won't have any leftover chicken on hand, or you want to try a recipe that calls for more cooked chicken than you are likely to have available.

How much will you need? The following chart will help you estimate how much chicken to buy when a recipe calls for cooked chicken. Quantities are approximate because the weight of uncooked chicken parts may vary slightly, and the ratio of meat to fat, skin, and bones will not always be exactly the same.

about 1/3 cup cubed cooked	1 boneless thigh
about 1/2 cup cubed cooked	1 boneless breast piece (1/2 breast)
about 3/4 cup cubed cooked	1 breast half with skin and ribs

about 2 1/2 cups cubed cooked	1 broiler fryer
about 5 cups cubed cooked	5 pound roaster
1 cup ground	1 cup cubed or diced cooked chicken

If you own a scale, it will help you to know that one cup of diced cooked chicken will weigh slightly less than five ounces. However, since some weight loss occurs during cooking, you will need at least six ounces of trimmed uncooked meat (skin and bones removed) to get one cup of diced cooked meat.

To grind chicken, cut cooked chicken into chunks and place in the container of a blender or food processor. Cover and process to the desired consistency. Don't overprocess the chicken because, if you do, you may get chicken purée. If you want to add additional ingredients to the chicken while it is still in the food processor or blender, add them before the chicken has been completely ground to avoid overprocessing.

Healthful Tips

When you cut or chop raw chicken on a work surface, bacteria remains on the counter or cutting board after the chicken has been removed. Therefore it is necessary to scrub the surface thoroughly before placing other food on the same surface. This is particularly important when it involves food that will be eaten uncooked, such as a salad or a sandwich. Scrub the surface very carefully with hot soapy water and wipe it dry with a clean cloth. A few drops of kitchen bleach added to the wash water will provide additional protection. Wooden work surfaces or chopping boards are particularly porous and require extra care to remove bacteria.

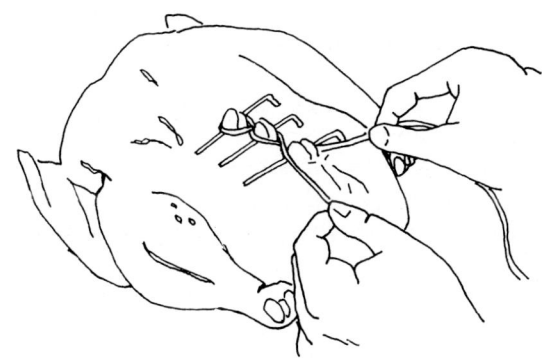

The cavity of a roast chicken provides a most hospitable climate for the growth of bacteria. This is why stuffing must

NEVER be placed inside the chicken until the chicken is ready to be placed in the oven. For the same reason, leftover stuffing should not be allowed to remain in roasted chicken. It should be removed and stored in a separate bowl in the refrigerator.

A meat thermometer will help you determine if your roast chicken and stuffing have been cooked long enough to reach the proper internal temperature for safe eating. In order to get an accurate reading from a meat thermometer, the thermometer must be inserted correctly (see illustration below). Insert the thermometer into the thickest part of the thigh, being careful not to let the tip of the thermometer touch a bone. When the temperature reaches 180°F, the chicken is done. To check stuffing, insert the thermometer into the center of the stuffing. The stuffing is done when the temperature reaches 165°F.

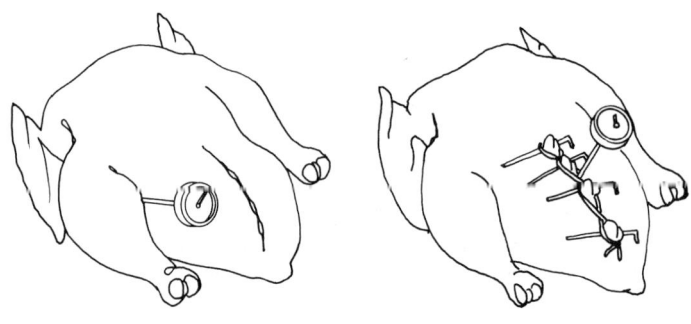

Increasing and Decreasing Recipes

Most of the recipes in this book can be increased or decreased easily, but there are obvious exceptions. If a five to six pound roaster is the correct amount to feed six people, you cannot adjust the recipe to feed ten, unless you are prepared to cook two roasters. On the other hand, it is good planning to cook a roaster that will feed six, use it to serve only four, and have planned leftovers that can be used in a variety of ways for another meal.

Good seasoning:

When you double a recipe, most of the ingredients can be doubled without difficulty. The exception is seasoning. In all probability, if you double the seasoning, you will have too much. It is also likely that you may not have enough seasoning if you reduce it too much when you decrease a recipe.

When adjusting quantities, the best rule to follow is to disregard seasoning amounts, and season to taste. You may find that, after you have decreased a recipe, you will still need the original 1/2 teaspoon of curry to get the proper curry flavor. But you may also find that twice the amount, or 1 teaspoon of curry, is entirely too much in a doubled recipe.

Trust your instincts and your taste buds. Start by adding only a small amount of seasoning and after you have tasted the food, add more if there is still not enough flavor. Once you have added too much seasoning, there is very little you can do to remedy the situation. If more flavor is needed, you can always add additional seasoning.

Good timing:

When you increase a recipe, you may need extra time to chop vegetables or brown or fry pieces of chicken. However, unless you are roasting chicken based on a specific number of minutes per pound, your cooking time probably will be unchanged if you are cooking by a conventional method. The amount of cooking time will be changed, however, if you use a microwave oven (see section on Microwave Cooking, page 96).

Good spacing:

It is important to avoid crowding food in a cooking utensil. If the volume of food is increased, be sure to use a pan or casserole large enough to allow the food to cook properly. Chicken that is sautéed or fried should always be cooked in small batches. You may find it necessary to use a small pan when a recipe is decreased so the food will not be lost in a large casserole or, if appropriate, will still be covered by cooking liquid. Estimate the volume of food you are going to cook and choose your pan size accordingly.

Planning a party?

Cooking for a crowd can present problems that normal cooking does not. Chicken is an ideal food to serve at a big party, but you must think through your choice of chicken recipes. Here are some important suggestions to make party giving as easy as possible:

1. Choose a recipe that can be prepared ahead of time.
2. Choose a recipe that does not call for too much time-consuming preparation.
3. Remember to process food in small batches so you don't overload your blender or food processor.

4. Use bowls, pans, and serving dishes large enough to accommodate increased quantities of food.
5. Provide enough refrigerator space to keep food fresh.
6. Make sure you have adequate facilities to reheat food or keep it warm until you are ready to serve it.

If you plan carefully, you can join the party and enjoy your favorite chicken recipe with your guests.

How To Microwave Chicken

Chicken lends itself very well to microwave cooking. Since this is a "moist" method of cooking, microcooked chicken is tender, juicy, and moist. The only disadvantage to cooking chicken in the microwave oven is that it is not possible to make the skin as crisp and brown as it can be made by conventional cooking methods. If your microwave oven has a browning unit, you will be able to add color to your chicken, but you will not be able to make the skin crisp. If you have a microwave/convection oven, you will be able to brown and crisp chicken without any difficulty.

Most chicken recipes can be cooked at 100% power (high) for 8 to 9 minutes per pound. However, cooking time is affected by two factors that must be taken into consideration whether you follow the suggested timing in a microwave recipe, or convert a conventional recipe.

1. The volume of food cooked in a microwave oven determines the amount of time necessary to cook it. The more food you place in the oven, the longer it will take to microcook. Therefore, if you are preparing a large casserole, or several casseroles, for company, you may find that conventional cooking will be just as quick as, or even quicker than, microcooking. On the other hand, if you want to cook just one breast or two drumsticks, they can be microcooked in just a few minutes. Don't forget that a large thick piece of chicken will cook more slowly than two thin pieces of chicken.
2. The temperature of food placed in a microwave oven will also affect the amount of time necessary to microcook it properly. Chicken that has just been thawed, or that is taken directly from the refrigerator, will take longer to microcook than chicken that is at room temperature or has been partially cooked.

Microcooking Hints and Tips:
• Whenever possible, use a round microproof dish rather than an oblong-shaped dish.

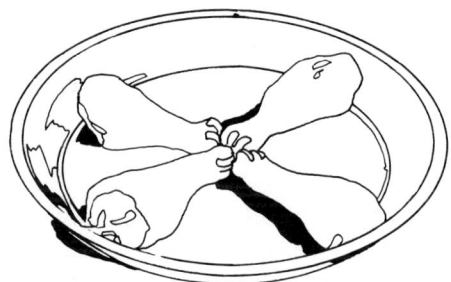

- Position the chicken in the dish with the thickest part of the chicken pieces at the outer edge of the dish. Microwaves cook from the outside in toward the center.
- Cover the dish loosely with plastic wrap or waxed paper to prevent food from splattering in the oven and to speed cooking. Turn one corner of the cover back to make a vent that will allow steam to escape. Cover breaded chicken with a paper towel. The paper towel will absorb some of the unwanted moisture and will prevent the crumbs from popping around inside the oven.
- To add appetizing color to microcooked chicken, sprinkle the chicken with paprika before cooking, or add a little browning sauce or soy sauce to melted butter or margarine and brush it over the surface of the chicken. If you use soy sauce, you may want to reduce or eliminate salt from the recipe.
- If your finished dish calls for cheese, add the cheese during the last few minutes of cooking.
- When you convert a conventional recipe to microwave cooking, reduce the liquid by one-third to one-half.
- Remember that, as with conventional cooking, white meat cooks more quickly than dark meat.
- Always check for doneness before you think the chicken is fully cooked. You can always cook it for a longer period, but once the chicken has been overcooked, there is nothing you can do about it.
- Take advantage of your microwave oven to heat leftovers and to reheat food when a member of the family is late for dinner. Place the chicken on a microproof plate, cover loosely, and reheat for just a few minutes at 70% power or at medium. Chicken reheated this way will not be dry.

Something For Nothing!

Delicious, flavorful chicken fat:

All too often cooks discard chicken fat because they are not aware of the many ways it can be used. But if you are watching your budget, or if you want to add chicken flavor to a recipe, you can take advantage of this special extra, found in almost every chicken. To begin with, it's free! In addition, it's full of wonderful chicken flavor.

Rendered (melted) chicken fat can be used in place of butter, margarine, or vegetable oil in almost any recipe where additional chicken flavor is appropriate. It can also be combined with butter, margarine, or vegetable oil to add a bit of extraordinary flavor to them.

It is easy to render chicken fat. Start by removing the extra fat from the chicken when you rinse it. If you are going to render the fat immediately, you have a choice of three methods:

1. Place the chicken fat in a heavy saucepan and cover it with water. Simmer gently, uncovered, until the water has evaporated and only the rendered fat remains. Watch carefully and add more water as necessary. Strain the fat, cool it completely, and place it in a rigid container in either the refrigerator or freezer, depending on how soon you plan to use it. Any water that may still be present will remain on the bottom of the container and the chicken fat will solidify above it. Rendered fat stored in the refrigerator will have a spreading consistency. Fat stored in the freezer will be hard.

2. Place the chicken fat in a skillet and cook it over very low heat until the fat has melted entirely. Strain it and store as above. This method is quicker than rendering fat in water, but the odor will permeate the house and the fat will tend to splatter during cooking. When you use this method, it is important to watch carefully in order to prevent the fat from burning.

3. If you have a microwave oven, place one cup of fat in a microproof dish that has a tight-fitting top. Cover and cook at 100% power for six to eight minutes, or until the fat has been rendered. Increase or decrease the cooking time, depending on the amount of fat to be rendered. Strain it and store as above.

Tasty tidbits:

With any of these methods, you can add diced onion and small pieces of chicken skin to turn out treats called "grebenes" or "chicken cracklins." When chicken fat is rendered in water, onion and chicken skin may be added to the saucepan with the fat. When the fat is rendered in the skillet or microwave oven, the onion and skin should be added after the fat has been rendered. Cook until onion is lightly browned, and the chicken skin is crisp.

These tasty tidbits may be eaten plain, with a little salt, or chopped and added to recipes such as chopped chicken liver. The cooked onion may be used in a recipe, or it can simply be a way to add flavor to the rendered fat, in which case it is discarded when the fat is drained.

If you don't want to render the fat immediately, store it in a covered container in the refrigerator for two to three days, or in the freezer for several months. You can add more fat to the container whenever you trim another chicken.

Chicken Equals Nutritional Bonuses!

Chicken is special:

The light, delicate taste of chicken does not provide any clue to the fact that chicken is a nutritional heavyweight.

Few people realize how high chicken rates when compared to other meat. It has exactly the same high-quality complete protein as red meat! In fact, there is no popular meat that surpasses the protein in chicken, and few that equal it. The only real difference is that chicken is "white" rather than "red" meat.

High quality protein:

We need high-quality protein for its essential amino acids, indispensable in building, maintaining, and replacing body tissue, muscles, and cells. The amino acid profile of chicken is well balanced, and the quality of it is equal to beef.

The following chart shows the protein and individual amino acid content of raw chicken (flesh only) and of raw beef (medium fat without bone). The figures are based on a few ounces of each kind of meat. Note that chicken contains more protein than an equal amount of beef.

Protein and Amino Acid Profile
Chicken and Beef

	Raw Chicken about 3.5 oz. 100 gr.	Raw Beef about 3.5 oz. 100 gr.
Protein	18.60 gm	18.03 gm
Tryptophan	.207 gm	.213 gm
Threonine	.767 gm	.804 gm
Isleucine	.924 gm	.952 gm
Leucine	1.350 gm	1.491 gm (AMINO
Lysine	1.509 gm	1.590 gm ACIDS
Methionine	.493 gm	.451 gm
Cystine	.249 gm	.230 gm
Phenylalanine	.721 gm	.748 gm
Tyrosine	.597 gm	.617 gm
Valine	.902 gm	1.010 gm

Recommended Daily Dietary Allowance
for Various Nutrients:

Percentage of RDA Contributed by Chicken Parts
with Meat and Skin

	1/2 breast (5 oz.)	1 drumstick (2 1/2 oz.)	1 thigh (3 1/3 oz.)	1 wing (1 3/4 oz.)	Livers (1 oz.)
Vitamin A	2.42	1.38	2.72	1.44	131.52
Thiamine	6.07	3.60	3.87	1.60	2.93
Riboflavin	7.24	7.65	8.47	2.53	36.94
Niacin	71.84	19.89	25.50	14.52	14.80
Iron	5.94	4.17	5.17	2.61	15.20
Calcium	1.60	.80	.90	.60	.30
Phosphorus	25.20	11.30	13.60	6.50	8.70
Protein	67.20	31.27	36.09	19.95	12.78

Evaluating Parts:

Various parts of a chicken differ in the amount of nutrients they contain. For example, one pound of boneless breast has about 97 grams of protein, while a pound of boneless drumsticks has approximately 90 grams. Chicken liver is loaded with Vitamin A. One ounce provides more than the Recommended Daily Dietary Allowance.

The following chart shows the protein, fat, calorie, and carbohydrate content of chicken parts.

Nutritive Breakdown by Parts
Chicken Parts, Raw, Edible Portions

	Protein (Gr.)	Fat (Gr.)	Calories	Carbohydrates (Gr.)
1/2 Breast about 5 oz.				
Meat and skin	30.24	13.41	250	—
Meat only, about 4 oz.	27.24	1.46	129	—
1 Drumstick				
Meat and skin about 2 1/2 oz.	14.07	6.34	117	—
Meat only, about 2 1/4 oz.	12.77	2.12	74	—
1 Thigh				
Meat and skin about 3 1/3 oz.	16.24	14.34	199	—
Meat only, about 2 1/2 oz.	13.56	2.70	82	—
1 Wing				
Meat and skin about 1 3/4 oz.	8.98	7.82	109	—
Meat only, about 1 oz.	6.37	1.03	36	—
Livers, about 1 oz.	5.75	1.23	40	1.09

Source: USDA Handbook 8-5 (1979)

Special Diets Can Be Delicious!

People on diets — low calorie, low fat, low cholesterol, and low sodium — find chicken one of the best foods available to maintain a special diet and still enjoy a flavorful and satisfying meal.

Low calorie diets:

Chicken is the ideal food for anyone who is counting calories. When chicken is compared with other popular meat, chicken ranks lowest in calories! A three-ounce portion of broiled chicken breast, skin removed, has only 97 calories. Even when the skin is left on, the calorie count is only 150. An equivalent serving of roast pork has 310 calories, hamburger has 245 calories, and other meat has an even higher calorie count.

It is easy to maintain the low calorie content of chicken when you cook it. The meat and skin of chicken are so flavorful already that the additional fat is not necessary for flavor when broiling or roasting. Low calorie ingredients like herbs, lemon juice, fresh vegetables, and fruit enhance the flavor of chicken and can be used in place of high calorie sauces. A low calorie chicken dinner, thoughtfully prepared, can be a dieter's delight.

Should skin be removed?

Consumers often ask if it is necessary to remove chicken skin when cooking for low calorie or low fat diets. The answer is "yes," but only if an extremely low fat content is desired. Chicken skin contains only 17.1 grams of fat per 100 grams of raw meat.

Low fat and low cholesterol diets:

Chicken is the perfect food for people on low fat diets, too. No meat is lower in fat content than chicken. But there is an even more beneficial aspect than the low fat content. The fatty acids contained in chicken are two-thirds unsaturated and only one-third saturated.

There is also a higher proportion of linoleic acid in chicken than there is in most other animal fats. Why is linoleic acid important? Because it is necessary for human growth and reproduction. When it is consumed as 25 percent or more of the fat, linoleic acid lowers blood cholesterol in adults under certain dietary conditions. This is one of the major reasons why chicken is such a desirable food on a cholesterol-modifying diet.

Low sodium diets:

Chicken is also suitable for use in low sodium diets. A 100-gram edible portion of raw chicken, without skin, contains only 68 milligrams of sodium for the light meat, and only 85 milligrams for the dark meat.

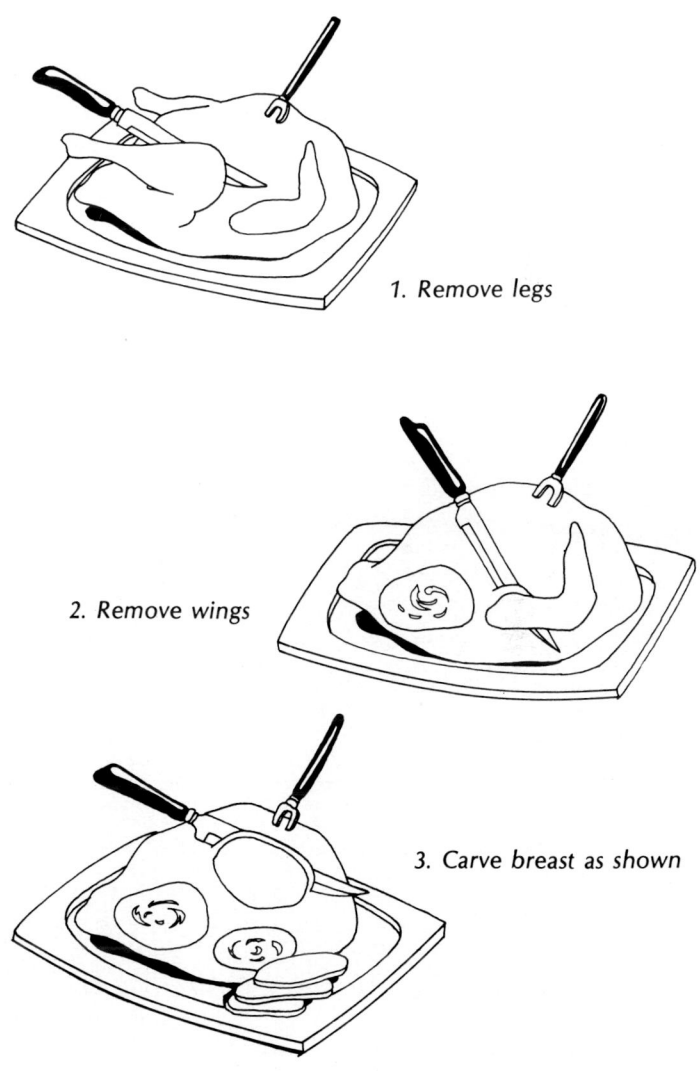

1. Remove legs

2. Remove wings

3. Carve breast as shown

Carving a chicken is easy when you follow the steps illustrated above.

Complete nutritional content:
You will appreciate the total nutritive value of chicken when you look at the following chart. It shows the complete nutritional content of chicken, plus the percentage of the Recommended Daily Dietary Allowance contributed by 3 1/2 ounces of cooked chicken.

Nutritive Content Of Chicken

Vitamins/ Minerals	RDA	3 1/2 ozs. (100 grams) roast chicken - average of white and dark meat	% of RDA for 3 1/2 ozs.
Vit. A	5,000 I.U.	105 I.U.	2.1%
Vit. C	60 mg	—	—
Thiamine	1.5 mg	.06 mg	4.0%
Riboflavin	1.7 mg	.17 mg	10.0%
Niacin	20mg	8.6 mg	43.0%
Calcium	1.0 grams	12 mg	1.2%
Iron	18 mg	1.5 mg	8.3%
Vit. D	400 I.U.	—	—
Vit. E	30 I.U.	—	—
Vit. B$_6$	2.0 mg	—	—
Folic Acid	.4 mg	—	—
Vit. B$_{12}$	6 micrograms	—	—
Phosphorus	1.0 grams	247 mg	24.7%
Iodine	150 micrograms	—	—
Protein	45 grams	29.8 grams	66.2%
Fat	—	4.9 grams	—
Carbohydrate	—	—	—
Calories	—	171	—

As the chart indicates, chicken is an excellent source of complete protein. This is the basic contribution to the diet. Chicken does not contain any carbohydrate or ascorbic acid, and it is low in iron, riboflavin, and thiamine. Chicken liver, however, is a rich source of Vitamin A and the B vitamins. It also has 8.47 milligrams of iron per 100 grams of cooked liver as compared to beef liver with only 6.5 milligrams per 100 grams.

California Avocado-Chicken Salad (page 106)
Chicken-Vegetable Mold (pages 106, 107)

Salads and Sandwiches

CALIFORNIA AVOCADO - CHICKEN SALAD
6 servings

3 cups cubed cooked
   chicken (page 93)
1 cup diced celery
1/2 cup coarsely chopped
   pecan halves, divided
2 large ripe avocados,
   divided
1/2 cup dairy sour cream

3 tablespoons lemon or
   lime juice, divided
1/2 teaspoon ground ginger
   salt and freshly ground
   pepper to taste
1 head Boston lettuce,
   washed and drained

Place chicken, celery, and 1/4 cup chopped pecans in bowl and toss lightly. Set aside. Cut 1 avocado in half and remove skin and pit. Dice and add to chicken mixture. Blend sour cream, 2 tablespoons lemon juice, ginger, salt, and pepper until well mixed. Pour dressing over chicken mixture and toss lightly. Cover and refrigerate until ready to serve. Line salad bowl with lettuce leaves. Place chicken salad in center of bowl. Peel and pit remaining avocado and cut into thin slices. Brush slices with remaining tablespoon lemon juice and garnish salad. Sprinkle remaining chopped pecans over salad and serve immediately.

CHICKEN-VEGETABLE MOLD
6 to 8 servings

1 package (6 ounces) lemon-
   or lime-flavored
   gelatin
2 cups boiling water
2 teaspoons lemon juice
1 1/2 cups diced cooked
   chicken (page 93)
1 cup diced peeled cucumber
1 cup diced red apple or
   pitted halved black
   grapes

1/2 cup finely chopped
   celery
1/3 cup thinly sliced
   scallions (green tops
   included)
   salt and freshly ground
   pepper to taste
   sprigs of watercress or
   parsley for garnish
   radish roses for
   garnish, (optional)

Dissolve gelatin in boiling water. Add 1 cup cold water and lemon juice and stir until blended. Refrigerate until slightly thickened. Combine chicken, cucumber, apple, celery, scallions, salt, and pepper, and fold into gelatin. Rinse 6 1/2-cup ring mold or decorative mold in cold water and spoon mixture into mold. Cover and refrigerate 4 to 5 hours or until set. Unmold onto serving dish. Garnish with sprigs of watercress and radish roses. Serve with mayonnaise or dairy sour cream.

NOTE: To make rooster shaped mold, divide mixture in half and spoon into two 3 1/2-cup rooster molds. Refrigerate until set.

GRAPEFRUIT AND CHICKEN SALAD

4 to 6 servings

2 cups cubed cooked
   chicken (page 93)
2 grapefruit, peeled, pits
   and membrane removed,
   divided into segments
1 cup cooked rice
1 large carrot, cut into
   julienne strips
1 small onion, minced
   salt and freshly ground
   pepper to taste

1 ripe avocado
   juice of 1 lemon
1/4 cup thousand island
   dressing
1/2 cup dairy sour cream or
   mayonnaise
1/2 teaspoon curry powder
   (optional)
   lettuce leaves

Place chicken, grapefruit segments, rice, carrot strips, and onion in bowl. Season with salt and pepper and mix well. Peel, pit, and cut avocado into cubes. Sprinkle with 1 tablespoon lemon juice, toss lightly, and add to chicken mixture. Blend remaining lemon juice, dressing, sour cream, and curry powder until well mixed. Arrange lettuce leaves on serving platter. Mound chicken mixture in center, spoon dressing over salad, and serve immediately.

WALDORF CHICKEN SALAD
WITH HONEY DRESSING *4 servings*

2 cups cubed cooked
  chicken (page 93)
2 medium-size red
  delicious apples,
  cored and diced
1 cup seedless green or
  pitted Tokay grapes,
  cut in half
1/2 cup coarsely chopped
  walnuts, divided

3 tablespoons honey
4 tablespoons lemon juice
1/4 cup vegetable oil
1/2 teaspoon tarragon
  salt and freshly ground
  pepper to taste
2 small heads Bibb lettuce
  or 2 Belgian endive

Place chicken, apples, grapes, and 1/4 cup chopped walnuts in medium-size bowl and toss gently. Place honey, lemon juice, oil, tarragon, salt, and pepper in screw top jar and shake vigorously until thoroughly blended. Pour dressing over chicken mixture and mix gently until all ingredients are coated. Cover and refrigerate. Just before serving, line salad bowl with lettuce and spoon chicken mixture into center. Sprinkle remaining chopped walnuts over salad and serve immediately.

SUMMER CHICKEN-ZUCCHINI
SALAD *4 to 6 servings*

4 tablespoons vegetable or
  olive oil, divided
3/4 pound small zucchini,
  trimmed and sliced
3 tablespoons lemon juice,
  divided
2 teaspoons curry powder
  salt and freshly ground
  pepper to taste

2 cups cooked rice
1/2 cup mayonnaise
2 1/2 cups cubed cooked
  chicken (page 93)
2 bananas
1/4 cup toasted shredded
  coconut for garnish

Heat 2 tablespoons oil in skillet, add zucchini, and sauté over high heat 4 minutes or until just tender. Remove zucchini with slotted spoon and drain on paper towels. Place remaining 2 tablespoons oil in large salad bowl. Add 1 tablespoon lemon juice, curry powder, salt, and pepper, and stir until blended. Add rice and stir to mix well. Add zucchini and toss gently. Blend mayonnaise with 1 1/2 tablespoons lemon juice, pour over chicken, and stir until well coated. Fold chicken into rice-zucchini mixture. Peel and slice bananas. Arrange banana slices on top of salad and sprinkle with remaining 1/2 tablespoon (1 1/2 teaspoons) lemon juice. Sprinkle coconut over salad and serve immediately.

HAWAIIAN HOT CHICKEN SALAD   *4 servings*

2 cups cubed cooked
chicken (page 93)
1 green pepper, seeded
and chopped
1/4 cup thinly sliced
scallions
1 can (8 1/4 ounces)
pineapple chunks,
syrup reserved
1/2 cup diced celery

1/2 cup coarsely chopped
macadamia nuts
salt and freshly ground
pepper to taste
1 tablespoon lemon juice
1/2 cup mayonnaise
1/4 teaspoon ground cumin
(optional)
shredded coconut for
garnish

Preheat oven to 375°F. Place chicken, green pepper, scallions, pineapple, celery, and macadamia nuts in bowl. Season with salt and pepper and mix well. Blend lemon juice, 1 tablespoon reserved pineapple syrup, mayonnaise, and cumin, and mix until well blended. Spoon over chicken mixture and stir gently. Transfer to 1-quart casserole, and bake 20 minutes or until heated through. Sprinkle with coconut and serve immediately.

Microwave Method: Prepare ingredients as directed above. Spoon chicken mixture into 1-quart microproof baking dish. Cover loosely and microcook at 100% power 4 to 5 minutes, stirring after 2 minutes. Serve as directed above.

CHICKEN FRANK AND
MACARONI SALAD   *8 servings*

1 package (16 ounces)
Holly Farms Chicken
Franks
1 cucumber, peeled,
seeded, and diced
1 onion, finely chopped
1 green pepper, seeded
and chopped
1 stalk celery, chopped
1 package (8 ounces)
elbow macaroni, cooked
according to package
directions

salt and freshly ground
pepper to taste
1 cup mayonnaise
2 tablespoons lemon juice
1/2 teaspoon celery seed,
crushed
1/2 teaspoon oregano
lettuce leaves
1 jar (2 ounces) sliced
pimientos, drained,
for garnish

Cut chicken franks into 1/2-inch thick slices and place in large bowl. Add cucumber, onion, green pepper, celery, macaroni, salt, and pepper, and mix well. Combine mayonnaise, lemon juice, celery seed, and oregano. Stir and fold into chicken frank mixture. Cover and refrigerate several hours. Line salad bowl with lettuce leaves and spoon salad into center. Garnish top with pimiento strips.

COLD CHICKEN WITH TUNANNAISE DRESSING

4 servings

8 Holly Farms Boneless
   Chicken Thigh Fillets
1 bay leaf
2 sprigs parsley
1 stalk celery, cut into
   chunks
6 to 8 peppercorns
1 teaspoon salt
1 cup mayonnaise
1 can (6 1/2 ounces) chunk
   light tuna, drained
2 teaspoons lemon juice

freshly ground pepper
   to taste
1 to 2 tablespoons drained
   capers, chopped
1 to 2 tablespoons milk
1 bunch watercress,
   washed and coarse
   stems removed, or
   shredded lettuce
2 hard-cooked eggs,
   sliced
paprika

Place thighs in medium-size saucepan with bay leaf, parsley, celery, peppercorns, and salt. Add enough water to cover and bring to a boil. Cover and simmer 16 to 18 minutes or until tender. Remove chicken with slotted spoon and set aside. Strain cooking liquid and reserve for use another time. Place mayonnaise, tuna, lemon juice, and pepper in container of blender or food processor and process to smooth purée. Spoon mixture into bowl, add capers and 1 tablespoon milk, and stir well. Add a little more milk if mixture is too thick. Arrange watercress on flat serving dish. Place chicken on top of watercress and surround with egg slices. Spoon Tunannaise Dressing over chicken and sprinkle with paprika. Refrigerate until ready to serve.

Microwave Method: Place thighs, bay leaf, parsley, celery, peppercorns, and salt in 1 1/2-quart microproof baking dish. Pour in enough water to cover, about 1 1/2 cups. Cover loosely and microcook at 100% power 12 to 14 minutes, turning thighs over after 6 minutes. Remove chicken with slotted spoon and set aside. Proceed as directed above.

CHILI-CHICKEN FRANKS   *8 servings*

1 package (16 ounces)
   Cheese Chicken Franks
   or Plain Chicken
   Franks
2 cups homemade chili or
1 can (16 ounces)
   chili

8 frankfurter buns
1/2 cup grated sharp Cheddar
   cheese (optional)
1 small onion, minced
   mustard, ketchup, and
   corn chips to serve

Place chicken franks in saucepan of boiling water and cook just until heated through. Remove from heat. Place chili in small saucepan and heat 3 to 5 minutes, stirring. Drain chicken franks and place 1 frank in each bun. Spoon chili over franks and sprinkle with cheese. Place filled buns on rack in broiler pan. Broil 2 to 3 minutes or until cheese is melted. Sprinkle with onion and serve with mustard, ketchup, and corn chips.

Microwave Method: Cut several diagonal slashes in each chicken frank. Set aside. Place chili in microproof bowl, cover loosely, and microcook at 100% power 2 1/2 to 3 minutes, stirring once. Remove from oven, keep covered, and set aside. Arrange 4 chicken franks, spoke fashion, on paper plate or microproof dish. Microcook at 100% power 2 minutes. Turn franks over and microcook at 100% power 1 minute. Place franks in buns, spoon chili over, and sprinkle with cheese. Microcook 4 franks in buns at 100% power 1 1/2 to 2 minutes or until cheese is melted. Repeat with remaining franks. Serve as directed above.

HOT 'N' SPICY FILLED POCKETS
4 servings

4 Holly Farms Boneless
  Chicken Breasts or
  6 to 8 Boneless Thigh
  Fillets
2 tablespoons butter or
  margarine
2 tablespoons dark brown
  sugar
1 small onion, minced
1 clove garlic, minced
3/4 cup ketchup
1 tablespoon Worcester-
  shire sauce

1 tablespoon white
  vinegar
1 1/2 teaspoons chili powder
  salt and freshly ground
  pepper to taste
  dash hot pepper sauce
4 large pita pockets,
  warmed
  lettuce leaves
8 slices tomato
1 green pepper, seeded
  and cut into 8 rings
  (optional)

Cut chicken into 1/2-inch cubes. Melt butter in large skillet, add chicken, and cook over high heat until lightly browned. Lower heat, add brown sugar, and stir until sugar is melted and chicken is coated. Add onion and garlic and cook until onion is transparent. Combine ketchup, 1/4 cup water, Worcestershire, vinegar, and chili powder in small bowl. Stir to blend. Add to skillet and stir well. Season with salt, pepper, and hot pepper sauce. Simmer, stirring until sauce is very thick, about 5 minutes. Split pita pockets in half crosswise and line each half with lettuce. Slice 2 tomato slices and 2 pepper rings into each pocket. Spoon chicken mixture into pockets and serve immediately.

Microwave Method: Cut chicken into 1/2-inch cubes. Place butter in shallow microproof baking dish and microcook at 100% power 1 minute. Add chicken and stir to coat. Cover and microcook at 100% power 4 minutes, stirring after 2 minutes. Remove chicken with slotted spoon. Add onion and garlic to dish, recover, and microcook at 100% power 3 minutes. Add brown sugar, ketchup, 2 tablespoons water, Worcestershire, vinegar, chili powder, salt, pepper, and hot pepper sauce. Stir well, recover, and microcook at 100% power 2 minutes. Add chicken and stir to coat. Recover and microcook at 100% power 2 minutes. Fill pockets as directed above.

Hot 'N' Spicy Filled Pockets,
Hot Chicken-Asparagus Open Sandwiches (page 116)

DARK AND LIGHT CLUB SANDWICHES

2 sandwiches

mayonnaise
4 slices white bread, toasted
2 slices whole-wheat bread, toasted
lettuce leaves
6 slices crisp-cooked bacon

4 slices tomato
4 large slices cooked chicken breast
salt and freshly ground pepper to taste
2 slices jellied cranberry sauce

Spread mayonnaise on 1 side of each piece of white toast and on both sides of whole-wheat toast. Place 1 slice white toast on plate, mayonnaise side up. Add a few lettuce leaves, cover with 3 bacon slices, and top with 2 tomato slices. Place 1 slice whole-wheat toast on top, cover with 2 chicken slices, season with salt and pepper, and add 1 slice cranberry sauce. Top with lettuce leaves and place 1 slice toast, mayonnaise side down, over lettuce. Repeat with remaining ingredients to make second sandwich. Cut each sandwich into 4 triangles. Insert long toothpicks into each triangle. Serve with additional mayonnaise on the side.

Variation: Substitute Russian dressing for mayonnaise.

NEW YORK CHOPPED LIVER SANDWICH

4 sandwiches

1 container Holly Farms
   Chicken Livers
3 tablespoons butter,
   margarine, or rendered
   chicken fat (page 98)
1 large onion, finely
   chopped
2 hard-cooked eggs

salt and freshly ground
   pepper to taste
1/4 to 1/3 cup mayonnaise
8 slices rye bread
   sliced red onion
   (optional)
   lettuce leaves

Rinse chicken livers under cold running water. Pat dry with paper towels and trim. Melt butter in skillet. Add onions and sauté 5 minutes or until transparent. Add livers and sauté 5 to 7 minutes or until livers are no longer pink. Either spoon liver-onion mixture into wooden bowl, add eggs, and chop; or place ingredients in container of food processor and process briefly to chop. (Do not purée.) Transfer to mixing bowl, and add salt, pepper, and just enough mayonnaise to moisten mixture and bind together. Cover and refrigerate several hours or until well chilled. Spread mayonnaise on bread and spread chicken liver mixture over mayonnaise. Top with sliced red onion, lettuce, and second slice of bread.

Microwave Method: Prepare chicken livers as directed above. Place butter in 1-quart microproof baking dish and microcook at 100% power 1 minute or until melted. Add livers and onion and stir well. Cover loosely and microcook at 100% power 7 minutes or until livers are no longer pink, stirring twice during cooking. Proceed as directed above.

Variation: Spread rendered chicken fat (page 98) on bread instead of mayonnaise.

HOT CHICKEN-ASPARAGUS OPEN SANDWICHES

4 sandwiches

2 tablespoons butter or
    margarine, softened
4 slices rye or
    pumpernickel bread,
    lightly toasted
8 to 12 slices cooked
    chicken breast

1 can (14 1/2 ounces)
    asparagus spears,
    drained
1/2 cup (8 tablespoons)
    grated sharp Cheddar
    cheese
paprika for garnish

Butter 1 side of each piece of toasted bread. Place 2 or 3 slices chicken on buttered side of each piece of toast. Divide asparagus spears equally and place on top of chicken. Place sandwiches on rack in broiler pan. Sprinkle each sandwich with 2 tablespoons grated Cheddar cheese. Broil about 4 minutes or until cheese is melted and golden brown. Sprinkle with paprika and serve immediately.

Microwave Method: Prepare sandwiches as directed above. Place 2 sandwiches on paper plate or paper towel and microcook at 100% power 1 to 1 1/2 minutes or until cheese is melted. Repeat with remaining 2 sandwiches. Serve as directed above.

FRIED BOLOGNA AND EGG SANDWICHES

4 sandwiches

1 to 2 tablespoons butter
    or margarine
8 slices Holly Farms
    Chicken Bologna
4 eggs

salt and freshly ground
    pepper to taste
4 crisp hard rolls or
8 slices bread
    ketchup

Melt butter in skillet. Add 2 to 3 slices chicken bologna and fry until browned on both sides. Remove and drain on paper towels. Fry remaining bologna, 2 or 3 slices at a time, drain, and set aside. Carefully break eggs into skillet. Season with salt and pepper. Cook eggs until whites are set and edges are lightly browned. Turn eggs over carefully with slotted spatula and cook until underside is done. Split rolls in half and spread each half with a little ketchup. Slide eggs onto bottom halves of rolls. Top each with 2 slices fried chicken bologna. Place tops of rolls over bologna and serve immediately.

CHICKEN BOLOGNA REUBEN SANDWICHES

4 sandwiches

2 tablespoons butter, softened

4 slices dark rye or pumpernickel bread, toasted

8 slices Holly Farms Chicken Bologna

8 tablespoons drained sauerkraut

4 tablespoons thousand island or Russian dressing

4 slices Swiss cheese

Lightly butter 1 side of each piece of toasted bread. Place 2 slices chicken bologna on buttered side of each piece of toast. Spoon 2 tablespoons sauerkraut onto each sandwich and dot each with 1 tablespoon dressing. Place 1 slice cheese on each sandwich and place sandwiches on rack in broiler pan. Broil 2 to 3 minutes or until cheese is melted. Serve immediately.

Microwave Method: Prepare sandwiches as directed above. Place 2 sandwiches on paper plate or paper towel and microcook at 100% power 1 1/2 to 2 minutes or until cheese is melted. Repeat with remaining 2 sandwiches. Serve immediately.

FRANKWICHES

8 servings

1 package (16 ounces) Holly Farms Chicken Franks

1 can (20 3/4 ounces) pork and beans

1 onion, minced

1/4 cup ketchup

1 teaspoon dry mustard

8 slices crisp-cooked bacon

8 soft buns

8 slices process American cheese (optional)

Preheat oven to 350°F. Cut chicken franks into small cubes and place in 1 1/2-quart baking dish. Add beans, onion, ketchup, and mustard, and stir until well mixed. Bake 30 to 35 minutes, stirring twice during cooking. Crumble bacon and stir into frank-bean mixture. Spoon frank mixture evenly onto bottoms of buns. Top each with slice of cheese and cover with top halves of buns. Serve immediately.

Microwave Method: Prepare ingredients as directed above. Spoon frank-bean mixture into 1 1/2-quart microproof baking dish. Cover loosely and microcook at 100% power 5 minutes. Stir, pushing franks down into beans. Recover and microcook at 100% power 7 to 8 minutes, stirring once. Crumble bacon and add to frank-bean mixture. Proceed as directed above.

CHICKEN "POPS"

4 to 6 servings

4 Holly Farms Boneless
Chicken Breasts or 6 to
8 Boneless Chicken
Thigh Fillets
1 cup pancake and waffle
mix
1 teaspoon salt
1/8 teaspoon pepper
1 egg, beaten
1 tablespoon vegetable oil
vegetable oil for
deep-frying
sweet and sour sauce or
honey to serve

Spread chicken breasts flat, place between 2 pieces of plastic wrap, and pound with meat mallet or rolling pin. Cut each breast into 5 or 6 pieces and set aside. Place pancake mix, salt, pepper, egg, 1 tablespoon vegetable oil, and 1/2 cup plus 2 tablespoons water in mixing bowl. Beat with wire whisk until batter is smooth. Refrigerate 15 to 20 minutes. Heat 2 to 3 inches oil in skillet or deep-fat fryer. Dip 1 piece chicken in batter, shake off excess, and carefully drop into moderately hot oil. Fry 3 or 4 pieces 2 minutes, turn, and fry 2 minutes or until golden brown all over. Remove from oil with slotted spoon and drain on paper towels. Repeat with remaining chicken pieces and batter. (Do not allow oil to get too hot or batter will cook too quickly and chicken will not be cooked through.) Insert a lollipop stick or long toothpick into each piece of chicken, season with additional salt if desired, and serve hot with sweet and sour sauce or honey.

Chicken "Pops"

Light Dishes
and Leftovers

CHICKEN CROQUETTES

4 servings

4 tablespoons butter or
  margarine
1/4 cup all-purpose flour
1 cup homemade chicken
  stock (page 24) or
  canned chicken broth
1 tablespoon freshly
  chopped parsley

1/2 teaspoon thyme
  salt and freshly ground
  pepper to taste
2 cups finely diced cooked
  chicken (page 93)
1 egg

Coating:

1 egg
  about 1/4 cup all-purpose
  flour, seasoned with
  salt and pepper to
  taste

3/4 cup dry bread crumbs
  vegetable oil for
  deep-fat frying

Melt butter in medium-size saucepan. Add flour and cook over low heat, stirring, 1 minute. Add stock and cook, stirring, until thickened. Remove from heat, add parsley, thyme, salt, and pepper, and stir well. Stir in chicken and set aside to cool slightly. Lightly beat egg and stir into chicken mixture until well blended. Transfer to bowl, cover, and refrigerate at least 2 hours. Cover wire rack with waxed paper and set aside. To make coating, beat egg in small bowl with 1 tablespoon water. Shape chilled chicken mixture into 8 croquettes or patties. Dredge each croquette in seasoned flour, dip into beaten egg, and roll in bread crumbs. Place on waxed paper-covered rack and let stand 30 minutes. Heat about 3 inches oil in deep-fat fryer. Fry 2 to 3 croquettes at a time, about 2 minutes on each side. Remove croquettes with slotted spoon and drain on paper towels. Serve hot with Pan Gravy (page 34).

CHICKEN FRITTERS

4 to 6 servings

2 cups diced cooked
    chicken (page 93)
1/3 cup minced green pepper
1 small onion, grated
2 eggs, separated
1/4 cup all-purpose flour

1 teaspoon baking powder
1/2 teaspoon salt
3 tablespoons butter or
    margarine
2 tablespoons vegetable
    oil

Combine chicken, green pepper, onion, and egg yolks in bowl and stir until well mixed. Stir flour, baking powder, and salt together, add to chicken mixture, and mix well. Beat egg whites until stiff. Stir heaping tablespoon into chicken mixture to lighten. Fold in remaining egg whites. Heat butter and oil in heavy skillet over moderate heat. Drop 2 or 3 heaping table-spoonfuls chicken mixture into skillet and cook 3 to 4 minutes on each side or until golden brown. Remove fritters with slotted spoon and drain on paper towels. Repeat with remaining chicken mixture, frying only 2 ot 3 fritters at a time. Serve hot with Pan Gravy (page 34), if desired.

CRISP-CHICKEN BAKE

4 servings

2 1/2 cups cubed cooked
    chicken (page 93)
1 can (10 3/4 ounces)
    condensed cream of
    chicken soup,
    undiluted
1/2 cup half and half or
    light cream
1/4 cup mayonnaise
2 tablespoons lemon juice
1 small onion, minced

2 stalks celery, finely
    chopped
1/3 cup sliced almonds
    salt and freshly ground
    pepper to taste
4 hard-cooked eggs, cut
    in half
1 1/2 to 2 cups crushed potato
    chips (plain or
    flavored)

Preheat oven to 350°F. Place chicken in lightly greased 1 1/2-quart casserole. Set aside. Combine soup, half and half, mayonnaise, and lemon juice in bowl, and stir until well blended. Add onion, celery, and almonds, and stir to mix. Season with salt and pepper. Spoon soup mixture evenly over chicken. Make 8 small indentations on top of sauce with back of tablespoon. Place 1 egg half, yolk down, in each indentation. Sprinkle top of casse-role with potato chips, covering completely. Bake 20 to 25 minutes or until hot and bubbly.

FAMILY CHICKEN AND RICE BAKE

4 servings

2 tablespoons butter or
   margarine
1 large onion, chopped
2 stalks celery, chopped
2 large carrots, thinly
   sliced
6 leaves Chinese cabbage
   or Iceberg lettuce,
   shredded
2 1/2 cups cubed cooked
   chicken (page 93)
1 can (15 ounces) whole
   peeled tomatoes,
   chopped

2 cups cooked rice
1 can (7 ounces) whole
   kernel corn, drained
2 tablespoons freshly
   chopped parsley
1/2 teaspoon thyme
   salt and freshly ground
   pepper to taste
1/2 cup grated Monterey
   Jack cheese

Melt butter in 2 1/2-quart flameproof casserole. Add onion, celery, carrots, and cabbage, and sauté until onion is transparent. Remove from heat. Preheat oven to 350°F. Add chicken, tomatoes, rice, corn, parsley, thyme, salt, and pepper. Stir well, sprinkle cheese over top, and bake 25 minutes or until hot and bubbly.

QUICK CHICKEN LO MEIN

4 servings

1 package (8 ounces) dried
   lo mein noodles
1/4 cup homemade chicken
   stock (page 24) or
   canned chicken broth
2 tablespoons soy sauce
1 teaspoon cornstarch
2 tablespoons vegetable
   oil

1 cup shredded Chinese or
   green cabbage
1 bunch scallions, thinly
   sliced (green tops
   included)
1 cup thinly sliced
   mushrooms
1 cup shredded cooked
   chicken (page 93)

Cook noodles in lightly salted boiling water until just tender. Drain and set aside. Blend stock, soy sauce, and cornstarch in small bowl. Stir until smooth and set aside. Heat oil in wok or large skillet. Add cabbage and stir-fry over high heat 4 minutes. Add scallions and mushrooms and stir-fry 2 to 3 minutes. Add chicken and reserved noodles and stir-fry 1 minute. Add reserved soy sauce mixture and cook 1 minute, stirring, until all ingredients are well coated. Serve immediately.

CHICKEN FRIED RICE

4 servings

4 tablespoons peanut oil
1 egg, lightly beaten
1 clove garlic, minced
1 bunch scallions, thinly
   sliced
1 cup shredded cooked
   chicken (page 93)

3 cups cooked rice
1 can (4 ounces) sliced
   mushrooms, drained
2 tablespoons soy sauce
   freshly ground pepper
   to taste

Heat oil in wok or large skillet. Add egg and cook over high heat, stirring constantly with fork. Add garlic and scallions, and stir-fry 1 minute. Add rice, chicken, mushrooms, soy sauce, and pepper, and stir well. Cook over moderate heat 4 to 5 minutes or until heated through. Serve immediately.

CHICKEN FOO YOUNG

4 to 6 servings

1 tablespoon cornstarch
1 1/2 cups homemade chicken
   stock (page 24) or
   canned chicken broth
4 teaspoons soy sauce,
   divided
1 1/2 cups bean sprouts (fresh
   preferred)
8 eggs
1 1/2 cups slivered cooked
   chicken (page 93)

1 bunch scallions, thinly
   sliced (green tops
   included)
1 stalk celery, cut into
   julienne strips
   salt and freshly ground
   pepper to taste
   peanut oil or vegetable
   oil for frying

Blend cornstarch, stock, and 2 teaspoons soy sauce in saucepan until smooth. Place saucepan over low heat and cook, stirring, until thickened and clear. Set aside and keep warm. Rinse bean sprouts under cold running water and drain well. Beat eggs in medium-size bowl, add bean sprouts, chicken, scallions, celery, remaining 2 teaspoons soy sauce, salt, and pepper, and mix well. Heat about 1/4 inch oil in heavy skillet. Use about 4 tablespoons egg mixture for each patty. Fry 1 or 2 patties at a time, about 5 minutes on each side or until golden brown. Drain on paper towels. Repeat with remaining egg mixture. Serve with reserved sauce.

CHICKEN AND MUSHROOM HASH *4 servings*

6 tablespoons butter or
  margarine, divided
2 tablespoons all-purpose
  flour
3/4 cup homemade chicken
  stock (page 24) or
  canned chicken broth
1/2 cup heavy cream
2 tablespoons dry sherry
  or dry white wine
  (optional)
  salt and freshly ground
  pepper to taste

1 onion, coarsely chopped
1/2 pound mushrooms, thinly
  sliced
1 green or red pepper,
  seeded and chopped
2 cups diced cooked
  chicken (page 93)
2 cups diced cooked
  potatoes
1/4 cup seasoned dry bread
  crumbs

Melt 2 tablespoons butter in saucepan. Add flour and cook over low heat, stirring, 1 minute. Add stock and cream slowly and cook, stirring, until mixture comes to a boil and thickens. Remove from heat, stir in sherry, salt, and pepper, and set aside. Preheat oven to 350°F. Melt remaining 4 tablespoons butter in skillet. Add onion, mushrooms, and green pepper, and sauté until onion is transparent. Combine chicken, potatoes, mushroom mixture, and 3/4 cup reserved sauce in shallow casserole and mix well. Pour remaining sauce on top, sprinkle with bread crumbs, and bake 30 to 35 minutes.

Microwave Method: Place 2 tablespoons butter in 4-cup glass measure and microcook at 100% power 1 minute. Stir in flour and microcook at 100% power 45 seconds. Stir in stock and cream slowly and microcook at 100% power 3 minutes, stirring once. Stir in sherry, salt, and pepper, and set aside. Place remaining 4 tablespoons butter in 2-quart microproof casserole and microcook at 100% power 1 minute or until melted. Add onion, mushrooms, and green pepper, and stir well. Cover and microcook at 100% power 4 minutes. Add chicken, potatoes, and reserved sauce, and mix well. Recover and microcook at 50% power 10 to 12 minutes or until heated through, stirring gently every 2 minutes. Brown bread crumbs in additional 2 tablespoons butter or margarine on top of range and spoon over casserole.

GUACAMOLE FRANKS

4 to 6 servings

1 ripe avocado
juice of 1/2 lemon
2 tablespoons mayonnaise
1/2 cup finely diced fresh
tomato
1 small onion, minced
1/2 teaspoon chili powder
salt and freshly ground
pepper to taste

hot pepper sauce to
taste
1 package Holly Farms
(16 ounces) Chicken
Franks
1 tablespoon butter or
margarine
8 frankfurter buns

Peel and pit avocado and scoop out flesh. Place in bowl and mash well. Add lemon juice and mayonnaise and stir until well blended. Add tomato, onion, chili powder, salt, pepper, and hot pepper sauce. Mix well, cover, and refrigerate until ready to serve. Split franks lengthwise, but do not cut all the way through. Heat butter in medium-size skillet. Add chicken franks and cook over moderate heat until heated through. Heat buns and place 1 chicken frank, split side up, on each bun. Spoon guacamole down center of franks.

SAUTEED CHICKEN LIVERS WITH ARTICHOKE HEARTS

4 servings

1 container Holly Farms
Chicken Livers
1/4 cup butter or margarine
1 large onion, sliced
1 clove garlic, minced
1 can (14 ounces) artichoke
hearts, drained and
cut into quarters
1/2 cup homemade chicken
stock (page 24) or
canned chicken broth

1/4 cup dry vermouth or
dry sherry
1 teaspoon marjoram
1/2 teaspoon thyme
salt and freshly ground
pepper to taste

Rinse chicken livers under cold running water. Pat dry with paper towels and cut in half. Melt butter in skillet, add onion and garlic, and sauté until onion is transparent. Add chicken livers and cook over moderate heat 5 to 6 minutes. Add artichoke hearts, stock, vermouth, marjoram, thyme, salt, and pepper. Cook 5 minutes, stirring occasionally, or until livers are cooked and artichoke hearts are heated through. Serve immediately.

EASY CREAMED CHICKEN
4 *servings*

1 can (10 3/4 ounces)
condensed cream of
chicken soup, undiluted
1/2 cup light cream
2 cups diced cooked
chicken (page 93)
1 can (4 ounces) sliced
mushrooms, drained

salt and freshly ground
pepper to taste
1/2 teaspoon paprika
2 tablespoons dry sherry
(optional)

Place soup and cream in saucepan over low heat. Cook, stirring, until mixture is smooth. Add chicken, mushrooms, salt, pepper, and paprika, and cook until heated through. Remove from heat and stir in sherry. Serve over hot cooked mashed potatoes, rice, or pasta; on English muffin halves or toast; or in baked patty shells.

Microwave Method: Place soup and cream in medium-size microproof bowl or 1 1/2-quart microproof casserole. Stir well, cover, and microcook at 70% power 5 to 6 minutes, stirring after 3 minutes. Add chicken, mushrooms, salt, pepper, and paprika, and stir well. Recover and microcook at 70% power 3 to 4 minutes or until heated through. Add sherry and serve as directed above.

CHICKEN LIVERS AND HAM IN PATTY SHELLS
6 *servings*

1 package (10 ounces)
frozen patty shells
6 tablespoons butter or
margarine, divided
2 tablespoons all-purpose
flour
1/2 cup homemade chicken
stock (page 24) or
canned chicken broth
1/2 teaspoon dry mustard
1 cup light cream or half
and half
salt and freshly ground
pepper to taste

1 container Holly Farms
Chicken Livers
1/2 cup finely chopped
onion
1/2 pound mushrooms, sliced
3/4 cup chopped cooked ham
1/2 teaspoon sage
(optional)
2 to 3 tablespoons dry
sherry or brandy
snipped chives for
garnish

Preheat oven to 425°F and prepare patty shells according to package directions. Keep warm. Melt 2 tablespoons butter in small saucepan. Add flour and cook 1 minute, stirring constantly. Pour in stock slowly and cook, stirring, until thickened and well blended. Add mustard and cream and cook over low heat, stirring, until sauce comes to a boil and is thickened. Season with salt and pepper and set aside. Rinse chicken livers under cold running water. Pat dry with paper towels and cut into 4 pieces. Melt remaining 4 tablespoons butter in large skillet. Add onion and mushrooms to skillet and sauté about 4 minutes. Add chicken livers to skillet and cook over low heat until livers are browned on all sides. Add ham and sage and stir well. Stir in reserved sauce slowly and cook 1 minute. Add sherry and cook over low heat 2 minutes or until heated through. Remove centers from baked patty shells. Spoon chicken liver mixture into shells. Sprinkle with chives and replace tops of patty shells. Serve immediately.

CHICKEN LIVER OMELET
4 servings

8 to 10 Holly Farms Chicken Livers
4 tablespoons butter or margarine, divided
1 clove garlic, crushed
1 small onion, minced
1/2 cup thinly sliced mushrooms
1/2 cup homemade chicken stock (page 24) or canned chicken broth
1 tablespoon dry sherry or dry white wine
1 tablespoon tomato paste salt and freshly ground pepper to taste
8 eggs
1 tablespoon freshly chopped parsley for garnish

Rinse chicken livers under cold running water and pat dry with paper towels. Trim livers and cut into small chunks. Melt 2 tablespoons butter in skillet. Add garlic and onion and sauté 1 minute. Add livers and mushrooms and cook 3 to 4 minutes. Remove liver-mushroom mixture with slotted spoon and set aside. Add stock to skillet and bring to a boil, scraping up browned particles on bottom of skillet. Boil rapidly until reduced by half. Add sherry and stir in tomato paste. Return liver-mushroom mixture to skillet, season with salt and pepper, and cook, stirring, until heated through. Set aside and keep warm. Beat eggs, salt, pepper, and 2 tablespoons cold water until blended. Melt remaining 2 tablespoons butter in large omelet pan or skillet. When butter is foamy, add eggs and cook over moderate heat, stirring lightly with fork. Cook until eggs are set and bottom of omelet is golden brown. Spoon liver-mushroom mixture over half of omelet and fold other half of omelet over filling. Slide omelet onto serving plate. Sprinkle with parsley, cut into wedges, and serve immediately.

127

BASIC CREPE BATTER FOR
CHICKEN CREPES
about 16 crêpes

1 cup plus 2 tablespoons
   all-purpose flour
1/2 teaspoon salt
3 eggs

1 1/2 cups milk
3 tablespoons melted
   butter

Place flour in mixing bowl and stir in salt. Beat eggs and milk until well blended. Slowly pour beaten egg mixture into flour, beating constantly with wire whisk. Continue beating until batter is smooth. Beat in melted butter until thoroughly blended. Pour into pitcher, cover, and refrigerate at least 1 hour.

Blender or food processor method: Place eggs and milk in container of blender of food processor, cover, and process until well combined. Add flour and salt and process until batter is smooth. Pour in melted butter slowly and process until thoroughly blended. Pour into pitcher, cover, and refrigerate at least 1 hour.

To make crêpes: Melt just enough butter (about 1 teaspoon) to cover bottom of 6- or 7-inch crêpe pan or skillet. Stir batter and spoon 3 tablespoons into pan, swirling batter to coat bottom of pan in thin layer. Cook over moderate heat 1 1/2 minutes. Turn crêpe over and cook 1 1/2 minutes. Slide cooked crêpe onto flat dish and make remaining crêpes, adding butter to crêpe pan as necessary. If batter begins to thicken, add a small amount of milk and stir well. If crêpes are not going to be used immediately, place a piece of waxed paper between each crêpe. Overwrap with plastic wrap and store in refrigerator or freezer until ready to fill.

Quick Dilly Chicken Crêpes (page 130)

FLORENTINE CHICKEN CREPES *6 to 8 servings*

3 tablespoons butter or margarine
1 large onion, finely chopped
1 cup thinly sliced mushrooms
2 cups diced cooked chicken (page 93)
1 package (10 ounces) frozen chopped spinach, cooked and well drained
1/4 teaspoon nutmeg
salt and freshly ground pepper to taste
1 can (10 3/4 ounces) cream of chicken or cream of mushroom soup, undiluted
1/2 cup heavy cream
1/4 cup mayonnaise or dairy sour cream
1 cup shredded Jarlsberg or Swiss cheese, divided
about 16 crêpes

Melt butter in skillet. Add onion and mushrooms and sauté until onion is transparent. Place in large bowl, add chicken, cooked spinach, nutmeg, salt, and pepper, and stir until well mixed. Set aside. Place soup in saucepan, stir in cream, and cook over low heat until blended. Add mayonnaise and 1/2 cup cheese, stir well, and cook until cheese is melted. Preheat oven to 375°F. Pour half the sauce into chicken-spinach mixture and stir to combine. Spoon about 3 tablespoons chicken mixture onto center of each crêpe. Roll or fold crêpes and place in single layer, seam side down, in shallow baking dish. Pour remaining sauce over crêpes and sprinkle with remaining 1/2 cup cheese. Bake 15 to 20 minutes or until heated through.

QUICK DILLY CHICKEN CREPES *6 to 8 servings*

1 can (10 3/4 ounces) cream of chicken or cream of celery soup, undiluted
2 cups dairy sour cream
1 tablespoon freshly chopped dill or 1 teaspoon dried dill
1 teaspoon paprika
salt and freshly ground pepper to taste
3 cups diced cooked chicken (page 93)
about 16 crêpes

Preheat oven to 350°F. Mix soup, sour cream, dill, paprika, salt, and pepper in bowl until thoroughly blended. Measure 1 1/2 cups sauce and set aside. Add chicken to sauce remaining in bowl and mix well. Spoon about 3 tablespoons chicken mixture onto center of each crêpe. Roll or fold crêpes and place in single layer, seam side down, in shallow baking dish. Pour reserved sauce over crêpes. Bake 15 to 20 minutes or until heated through. Sprinkle with additional freshly chopped dill if desired and serve immediately.

CHICKEN AND SHRIMP CREPES *6 to 8 servings*

- 6 **tablespoons butter or margarine, divided**
- 2 **tablespoons minced shallots or 1 small onion, minced**
- 1 **cup thinly sliced mushrooms**
- 1 1/2 **cups diced cooked chicken (page 93)**
- 1 **cup diced cooked shrimp (6 to 8 large shrimp)**
- 1/2 **cup frozen tiny peas, thawed**
  salt and freshly ground pepper to taste
- 4 **tablespoons all-purpose flour**
- 1 **cup homemade chicken stock (page 24) or canned chicken broth**
- 1 **cup milk**
- 2 **tablespoons dry sherry**
- 2 **egg yolks, beaten**
- 1/2 **cup grated Parmesan cheese, divided**
  about 16 crêpes
- 1 **to 2 tablespoons freshly chopped parsley for garnish**

Melt 2 tablespoons butter in small skillet. Add shallots and mushrooms and sauté until softened. Place in large bowl, add chicken, shrimp, peas, salt, and pepper, and mix well. Set aside. Melt remaining 4 tablespoons butter in saucepan. Add flour and cook 1 minute, stirring constantly. Add stock and milk slowly and cook over low heat, stirring, until mixture thickens and comes to a boil. Stir in sherry. Spoon a little hot sauce into beaten egg yolks and stir. Pour egg yolk mixture back into saucepan. Add 1/4 cup cheese and cook over low heat, stirring until cheese is melted. (Do not allow mixture to boil.) Remove from heat and stir 1 1/4 cups sauce into chicken mixture. Preheat oven to 375°F. Spoon about 3 tablespoons chicken mixture onto center of each crêpe. Roll or fold crêpes and place in single layer, seam side down, in shallow baking dish. Pour remaining sauce over crêpes and sprinkle with remaining 1/4 cup cheese. Bake 15 to 20 minutes or until heated through. Sprinkle with parsley, serve immediately.

CHICKEN LIVER AND MUSHROOM CREPES

6 to 8 servings

1 container Holly Farms Chicken Livers
1/4 cup butter or margarine
1 bunch scallions, thinly sliced
1/2 pound mushrooms, thinly sliced
1 tablespoon freshly chopped parsley
1/2 teaspoon thyme
salt and freshly ground pepper to taste

1/4 cup dry sherry or dry white wine
1 cup homemade chicken stock (page 24) or canned chicken broth
1 tablespoon cornstarch
about 16 crêpes
1 cup shredded Gruyère or Swiss cheese

Rinse chicken livers under cold running water and pat dry with paper towels. Trim livers and cut into small cubes. Melt butter in large skillet. Add scallions and sauté until softened. Add chicken livers and cook, stirring, until livers are no longer pink. Add mushrooms and cook about 5 minutes. Add parsley, thyme, salt, pepper, and sherry, and simmer 3 minutes stirring occasionally. Remove from heat. Blend stock and cornstarch until smooth. Return skillet to low heat, add stock mixture, and cook, stirring, until thickened. Add a little more stock if mixture seems too thick. Preheat oven to 350°F. Spoon about 3 tablespoons chicken liver mixture onto center of each crêpe. Roll or fold crêpes and place in single layer, seam side down, in shallow baking dish. Sprinkle with cheese and bake 15 to 20 minutes or until cheese is melted and lightly browned.

CHICKEN AND HAM QUICHE

6 to 8 servings

pastry for 9-inch single crust pie
2 tablespoons butter or margarine
1 bunch scallions, sliced (green tops included)
3 eggs
1 1/2 cups light cream or half and half
1/4 teaspoon ground nutmeg

salt and freshly ground pepper to taste
1 cup grated Gruyère or Swiss cheese, divided
1 cup diced cooked chicken (page 93)
1 cup diced cooked ham
1 jar (2 ounces) sliced pimientos, drained

Preheat oven to 400°F. Use pastry to line 9-inch quiche pan or pie plate. Line pastry with foil and weigh down with dried beans, rice, or pie weights. Bake 8 minutes. Remove foil and weights and bake 5 minutes. Remove from oven and cool on wire rack. Lower oven temperature to 375°F. Melt butter in skillet, add scallions, and sauté until softened. Remove from heat and set aside. Beat eggs, half and half, nutmeg, salt, and pepper until well blended. Sprinkle 1/4 cup cheese in bottom of cooled crust. Spoon reserved scallions over cheese. Scatter chicken and ham over scallions. Top with pimientos. Carefully pour beaten egg mixture into crust and sprinkle remaining 3/4 cup cheese on top. Bake 35 to 40 minutes or until top is golden brown and center is set. Cool on wire rack 10 to 15 minutes before serving.

HOT CHICKEN SOUFFLE
4 servings

2 tablespoons butter or margarine	1 cup finely ground cooked chicken (page 93)
4 tablespoons all-purpose flour	1 tablespoon grated orange rind
1 1/4 cups homemade chicken stock (page 24) or canned chicken broth	salt and freshly ground pepper to taste
3 egg yolks	4 egg whites, room temperature

Lightly grease 1 1/2-quart soufflé dish and set aside. Melt butter in medium-size saucepan. Add flour and cook, stirring, 1 minute. Add chicken stock slowly and cook over low heat, stirring, until thickened. Lightly beat egg yolks. Spoon a little hot sauce into beaten egg yolks and stir. Pour egg yolk mixture back into saucepan. Cook over low heat or until thickened. (Do not allow mixture to boil.) Remove from heat and add chicken, orange rind, salt, and pepper. Stir until well blended. Preheat oven to 350°F. Beat egg whites until stiff. Stir heaping table-spoon into chicken mixture to lighten. Fold in remaining egg whites. Spoon chicken mixture into prepared soufflé dish and bake 40 to 50 minutes or until puffed and golden brown. Serve immediately with crisp green salad and warm dinner rolls.

Variation: Herbed Chicken Soufflé: Omit orange rind and add 1 tablespoon freshly chopped parsley, 1/2 teaspoon tarragon, and 1/4 teaspoon thyme. Proceed as directed above.

FAMILY-STYLE CHICKEN POT PIE

2 pies
6 servings each

4 cups diced peeled potatoes	salt and freshly ground pepper to taste
7 tablespoons butter or margarine, divided	1 cup heavy cream
2 large onions, chopped	1 package (10 ounces) frozen peas and carrots
1/2 pound mushrooms, thinly sliced	5 cups diced cooked chicken (page 93)
5 tablespoons all-purpose flour	pastry for two 9-inch pie crusts
2 1/2 cups milk	1 egg beaten with 1 tablespoon milk
1 1/2 cups homemade chicken stock (page 24) or canned chicken broth	

Cook potatoes in lightly salted boiling water until almost tender. Drain and place in large bowl. Melt 3 tablespoons butter in large saucepan. Add onions and mushrooms and sauté until onions are transparent. Remove from heat and add to bowl. Add remaining 4 tablespoons butter to saucepan and melt. Add flour and cook over low heat 1 minute, stirring constantly. Add milk and stock slowly and cook, stirring, until sauce is thickened and comes to a boil. Season with salt and pepper, add cream, and cook 1 minute. Stir peas and carrots into sauce. Add chicken to potato mixture, pour sauce over, and mix well. Divide mixture evenly in 2 deep 9-inch pie plates or 2-quart casseroles. Preheat oven to 400°F. Roll out pastry, 1 piece at a time, on lightly floured surface to 1 1/2 inches larger than rim of pie plate. Place pastry over chicken filling. Trim pastry edge, leaving 1-inch overhang. Fold overhang under and crimp or flute pastry edge. Cut several vents in pastry to allow steam to escape. Cut decorative shapes from pastry trimmings. Brush undersides of pastry shapes with water and place on top of crust to decorate pie. Repeat with remaining pastry. Brush tops of pies with beaten egg mixture. Place pies on large cookie sheet and bake 25 to 30 minutes or until pastry is golden brown. Remove pies and cool on wire rack 10 to 15 minutes. Serve 1 for dinner. Cool remaining pie completely and open freeze. When frozen, overwrap with aluminum foil and return to freezer. To serve, thaw and reheat in 350°F oven until hot and bubbly. If desired, freeze pie unbaked. Thaw and bake as directed above, or bake frozen about 1 hour.

Variation: Substitute 1 package (17 1/4 ounces) frozen puff pastry, thawed, for regular pie crusts.

Family-Style Chicken Pot Pie, Chicken Stuffed Tomatoes (page 136)

CHICKEN STUFFED TOMATOES   *4 servings*

4 **large, firm, ripe tomatoes**	**freshly ground pepper to taste**
salt to taste	1 **jar (2 ounces) sliced pimientos, drained (optional)**
2 **cups diced cooked chicken (page 93)**	**tiny parsley sprigs for garnish**
1 **cup finely chopped celery**	
1/2 **cup mayonnaise**	
1/2 **cup bottled French dressing**	

Hollow out tomatoes, discarding pulp and seeds. Sprinkle insides of tomatoes with salt, invert onto paper towels, and let drain 20 minutes. Refrigerate tomato shells. Combine chicken, celery, mayonnaise, French dressing, salt, and pepper, and mix well. Refrigerate chicken mixture until ready to serve. To serve, fill tomato cavities with chicken mixture. Arrange pimiento strips on top of chicken salad and garnish with tiny parsley sprigs.

CHICKEN MOUSSE   *6 to 8 servings*

1 **envelope unflavored gelatin**	1 **tablespoon grated onion**
3/4 **cup homemade chicken stock (page 24) or canned chicken broth, divided**	2 **teaspoons Worcestershire sauce**
	1/2 **teaspoon salt**
	1/8 **teaspoon cayenne**
2 **cups ground or finely diced cooked chicken (page 93)**	1/2 **cup mayonnaise**
	1 **cup heavy cream**
1/4 **cup minced celery**	**thin cucumber slices, pimiento strips, and parsley sprigs for garnish**
1/4 **cup finely chopped sweet gherkin pickles**	

Soak gelatin in 1/4 cup stock 5 minutes. Bring remaining 1/2 cup stock to a boil in small saucepan. Add gelatin and stir until gelatin is completely dissolved. Refrigerate until slightly thickened. Combine chicken, celery, pickle, grated onion, Worcestershire, salt, and cayenne in large bowl. Fold mayonnaise and reserved gelatin into chicken mixture until well blended. Whip cream until firm and fold into chicken mixture. Rinse 6-cup decorative mold in cold water. Spoon chicken mixture into mold. Cover and refrigerate several hours or until set. Unmold onto serving plate and garnish with cucumber slices, pimiento strips, and parsley sprigs.

Chicken Jambalaya (page 138),
Devilish Drumsticks (pages 138, 139)

Cooking for a Crowd—
Or One or Two

CHICKEN JAMBALAYA
10 to 12 servings

1/4 cup butter or margarine
2 packages Holly Farms
    Best of the Fryer
2 cups diced cooked ham
2 cloves garlic, minced
1 1/2 cups chopped onions
1 cup chopped green
    pepper
1 can (28 ounces)
    tomatoes, undrained
2 1/2 cups homemade chicken
    stock (page 24) or
    canned chicken broth
1/2 teaspoon thyme
1/4 teaspoon cayenne
2 bay leaves
    salt and freshly ground
    pepper to taste
1 pound medium-size
    shrimp, shelled and
    deveined
2 cups rice
2 tablespoons freshly
    chopped parsley

Melt butter in large Dutch oven. Add chicken pieces in 2 batches and brown on all sides. Remove chicken with slotted spoon and set aside. Add ham, garlic, onions, and green pepper to pan, and sauté until onions are transparent. Place tomatoes in bowl and break up with back of spoon. Add stock, thyme, and cayenne, and stir well. Add tomato mixture and bay leaves to pan, cover, and bring to a boil slowly. Add chicken and season with salt and pepper. Recover and simmer 30 minutes. Add shrimp, rice, and parsley, and stir well. Recover and simmer 20 to 25 minutes or until rice is cooked and chicken is tender.

NOTE: This dish can be made ahead of time and refrigerated. Cover and reheat in preheated 350°F oven 20 to 25 minutes or until heated through.

DEVILISH DRUMSTICKS
18 to 22 servings

36 Holly Farms Chicken
    Drumsticks
1 1/2 cups finely chopped
    onions
1/2 cup firmly packed
    brown sugar
3/4 cup lemon juice
3/4 cup soy sauce
1/2 cup vegetable oil
1/2 cup red plum,
    blackberry, or
    boysenberry jam
3 teaspoons ground
    coriander
3/4 teaspoon hot pepper
    sauce or to taste
    freshly ground pepper
    to taste
    lemon or lime slices
    and parsley sprigs for
    garnish

Cut 2 or 3 slashes in each drumstick. Arrange drumsticks in single layer in shallow glass baking dishes. Combine onions, brown sugar, lemon juice, soy sauce, oil, jam, coriander, hot pepper sauce, and pepper in bowl, stirring until well blended. Pour over drumsticks, turning to coat evenly. Cover and let stand at room temperature 1 hour 30 minutes, turning drumsticks occasionally. Preheat oven to 350°F. Uncover and bake 50 minutes or until tender, turning and brushing drumsticks with sauce at least once or twice during cooking. Arrange drumsticks on large serving platter and garnish with lemon slices and parsley sprigs. Serve warm or at room temperature.

CHICKEN TETRAZZINI

10 to 12 servings

1 cup (16 tablespoons) butter or margarine, divided
1 1/2 pounds mushrooms, thinly sliced
1/2 cup all-purpose flour
4 cups homemade chicken stock (page 24) or canned chicken broth
1 cup heavy cream
2 egg yolks
1 cup dry sherry or dry white wine

2 cups freshly grated Parmesan cheese, divided
salt and freshly ground pepper to taste
5 to 6 cups diced or slivered cooked chicken (page 93)
1 pound very thin spaghetti, cooked (vermicelli, angel hair, or spaghettini)

Melt 1/2 cup (8 tablespoons) butter in large skillet. Add mushrooms and sauté until lightly browned. Remove from heat and set aside. Melt remaining 1/2 cup (8 tablespoons) butter in large saucepan. Add flour and cook 2 minutes, stirring constantly. Add stock and cream slowly and cook over low heat, stirring, until thickened. Beat egg yolks and slowly stir in about 4 tablespoons hot sauce. Pour egg yolk mixture back into sauce, add sherry and 1 cup cheese, and cook over low heat, stirring, just until cheese is melted. Season with salt and pepper. Remove from heat and stir in reserved mushrooms. Remove 1 1/2 cups sauce and set aside. Preheat oven to 375°F. Add chicken and spaghetti to remaining sauce and stir until well mixed. Spoon mixture into large shallow casserole. Pour reserved sauce over top and sprinkle with remaining 1 cup cheese. Bake 15 to 20 minutes or until hot and bubbly. Place under broiler to lightly brown top. Serve hot.

CHICKEN DIVAN

18 to 22 servings

18 Holly Farms Chicken Breast Halves with Ribs
1 large onion, cut into quarters
1 tablespoon salt
8 black peppercorns
6 packages (10 ounces each) frozen broccoli spears or 3 bunches fresh broccoli
3/4 cup butter or margarine
3/4 cup all-purpose flour
3 cups homemade chicken stock (page 24) or canned chicken broth

3 cups milk
3/4 cup dry white wine or dry sherry
1 tablespoon Worcestershire sauce
1 teaspoon nutmeg
salt and white pepper to taste
1 1/2 cups grated Parmesan cheese, divided
1 cup heavy cream

Place chicken breasts, onion, salt, and peppercorns in large stockpot. Add enough cold water to cover. Bring to a boil, cover, and simmer 30 to 35 minutes or until chicken is tender. Remove chicken breasts with slotted spoon and let cool. When cool, remove and discard skin and bones. Slice chicken and set aside. Cook frozen broccoli until barely tender, or wash and trim fresh broccoli, divide into spears, and cook in lightly salted boiling water until barely tender. (Do not overcook.) Drain well and set aside. Melt butter in large saucepan. Add flour and cook 2 minutes, stirring. Add stock and milk slowly and cook over low heat, stirring until sauce is thickened and comes to a boil. Stir in wine, Worcestershire, nutmeg, salt, pepper, and 3/4 cup cheese. Cook, stirring, just until cheese is melted. Remove sauce from heat and set aside to cool. Preheat oven to 400°F. Lightly grease shallow casserole or two 13×9-inch baking dishes. Arrange broccoli spears in single layer in bottom of prepared dish. Sprinkle with a little reserved cheese. Top with chicken slices. Whip cream until firm, fold into sauce, and pour over chicken. Sprinkle with remaining cheese. Bake 20 minutes or until hot and bubbly. Place dish under broiler briefly to brown lightly on top.

Variation: Substitute cooked, fresh frozen or canned asparagus spears for broccoli.

Hint: This dish can be made ahead of time and refrigerated up to 2 days. Bring to room temperature before baking and increase baking time as necessary to heat thoroughly.

MELON-CHICKEN SALAD
2 servings

2 to 3 tablespoons
raisins
1 medium-size cantaloupe
1 cup diced cooked
chicken (page 93)
1/2 cup chopped green pepper
1/4 cup chopped walnuts

1/4 cup mayonnaise
2 tablespoons orange
juice
salt and freshly ground
pepper to taste
freshly chopped parsley
for garnish

Place raisins in small bowl, cover with warm water, and set aside. Cut cantaloupe in half, scrape out seeds, and invert onto paper towels to drain. Combine chicken, green pepper, and walnuts in bowl. Drain raisins, add to chicken mixture, and mix. Blend mayonnaise with orange juice, pour over chicken mixture, and stir to combine. Season with salt and pepper. Spoon chicken salad into cantaloupe halves and refrigerate until ready to serve. Sprinkle with parsley just before serving.

BUFFET CHICKEN SALAD
20 to 22 servings

10 cups cubed cooked
chicken (page 93)
3 cups diced celery
1 cup diced green or red
pepper
2 bunches scallions,
thinly sliced (green
tops included)
3 to 4 cups seedless
green grapes
1 1/2 cups coarsely chopped
nuts (salted almonds,
cashews, pecans, or
walnuts)

3 cups mayonnaise
1 1/2 cups dairy sour cream
1/2 cup cider or tarragon
vinegar
1 tablespoon sugar
hot pepper sauce
salt and freshly ground
pepper to taste
lettuce leaves
2 ripe avocados
lemon juice
cherry tomatoes

Combine chicken, celery, green pepper, scallions, grapes, and nuts in very large bowl and mix gently. Place mayonnaise in separate bowl and stir in sour cream until smooth. Add vinegar, sugar, a few drops hot pepper sauce, salt, and pepper, and stir until well blended. Pour dressing over chicken mixture and toss gently until all ingredients are well coated. Cover and refrigerate until ready to serve. To serve, line large salad bowl with lettuce leaves and spoon chicken salad into center of bowl. Peel, pit, and slice avocados. Brush slices with lemon juice. Garnish with avocado slices and cherry tomatoes.

141

CHICKEN LEGS IN
MUSHROOM SAUCE

2 servings

2 **Holly Farms Prime Chicken Legs**
   salt and freshly ground pepper to taste
2 **tablespoons butter or margarine**
1 **tablespoon vegetable oil**
1/4 **pound mushrooms, thinly sliced**
1 **tablespoon minced shallots or onion**
1 1/2 **tablespoons all-purpose flour**

1 **cup homemade chicken stock (page 24) or canned chicken broth**
1 **teaspoon browning sauce (optional)**
2 **tablespoons dry sherry or dry white wine**
   hot cooked noodles
1 **tablespoon freshly chopped parsley for garnish**

Season chicken with salt and pepper. Melt butter and oil in skillet. Add chicken and brown well on all sides. Remove chicken and set aside. Add mushrooms and shallots to skillet and sauté 3 minutes. Stir in flour and cook over low heat 1 minute, stirring. Stir in stock slowly and cook over low heat until thickened. Add browning sauce. Return chicken to skillet, cover, and simmer 25 to 30 minutes or until chicken is tender, turning occasionally. Stir sherry into sauce and adjust seasoning. Place noodles on serving platter. Top with chicken, spoon sauce over, and sprinkle with parsley. Serve immediately.

Microwave Method: Place butter and oil in microproof casserole. Cover loosely and microcook at 100% power 1 minute. Add mushrooms and shallots, cover, and microcook at 100% power 3 minutes, stirring after 1 1/2 minutes. Stir in flour. Add 3/4 cup stock slowly and stir until smooth. Recover and microcook at 100% power 3 minutes. Season chicken with salt and pepper and brush with 1 tablespoon browning sauce. Arrange chicken legs in casserole, placing thickest part of chicken at outer edge of dish. Spoon sauce over, recover, and microcook at 100% power 8 minutes. Turn chicken over, baste with sauce, recover, and microcook at 100% power 6 to 7 minutes or until tender. Serve as directed above.

KENTUCKY BURGOO

10 to 12 servings

1 Holly Farms Roaster or
  large Fryer
1 pound boneless beef
  for stew
2 smoked ham hocks (about
  1 1/2 pounds)
2 teaspoons salt
  freshly ground pepper
  to taste
1/4 teaspoon cayenne
1 large clove garlic,
  minced
2 cups diced potatoes
2 cups diced carrots
1 cup chopped onions
1 cup chopped celery
1 package (10 ounces)
  frozen baby lima beans

1 can (28 ounces) whole
  peeled tomatoes,
  coarsely chopped
1 bay leaf
1 cup fresh or frozen
  whole corn kernels
1 cup chopped green pepper
1 tablespoon Worcester-
  shire sauce
1/2 pound fresh okra,
  trimmed and sliced or
  1 package (10 ounces)
  frozen cut okra
1/2 cup freshly chopped
  parsley

Place chicken, beef cubes, and ham hocks in large stockpot or Dutch oven. Add salt, pepper, cayenne, and 12 cups water. Cover and bring to a boil, skimming surface as necessary. Lower heat and simmer, covered, 1 1/2 to 2 hours or until meat is tender. Remove meat from pot and set broth aside to cool. When broth is cool, skim fat from surface. Remove skin and bones from chicken and cut meat into cubes. Remove skin, fat, and bones from ham hocks and dice meat. Measure 10 cups broth and return broth to clean stockpot. Bring to a boil, lower heat, add garlic, potatoes, carrots, celery, onion, lima beans, tomatoes and their juice, and bay leaf, and simmer 20 minutes. Add chicken, beef cubes, ham, corn, green pepper, Worcestershire, and okra. Cook, stirring occasionally, 15 to 20 minutes or until vegetables are cooked and stew is thickened. Remove from heat, discard bay leaf, and stir in parsley. Serve hot with hot corn bread and a crisp salad.

143

MID-EASTERN CHICKEN

2 servings

2 large Holly Farms
  Boneless Chicken
  Breasts or 4 Boneless
  Chicken Thigh Fillets
2 tablespoons butter or
  margarine
1 tablespoon vegetable oil
1 small onion, chopped
1/4 cup diced celery
2 teaspoons all-purpose
  flour
2 teaspoons curry powder

1/8 teaspoon ground cloves
3/4 cup homemade chicken
  stock (page 24) or
  canned chicken broth
1 tart apple, peeled,
  cored, and diced
2 tablespoons raisins
1 tablespoon lemon juice
1 teaspoon grated lemon
  zest
salt and freshly ground
  pepper to taste

Cut chicken into thin slivers. Melt butter and oil in skillet. Add chicken and sauté over high heat about 3 to 4 minutes, stirring constantly, or until chicken is no longer pink. Remove chicken with tongs and set aside. Add onion and celery to skillet and sauté until onion is transparent. Add flour, curry powder, and cloves to skillet and cook over low heat 1 minute, stirring. Add stock slowly and cook over low heat, stirring, until sauce is thickened and comes to a boil. Add apple, raisins, lemon juice, and zest, and simmer 3 minutes. Add reserved chicken, salt, and pepper, and simmer 5 minutes, stirring occasionally. Serve over hot cooked rice.

Microwave Method: Cut chicken into thin slivers. Place butter and oil in 1 1/2-quart microproof baking dish and micro-cook at 100% power 1 minute. Add chicken and stir well to coat. Cover loosely and microcook at 100% power 3 minutes or until chicken is no longer pink, stirring after 1 1/2 minutes. Remove chicken with slotted spoon and set aside. Add onion and celery to dish, cover loosely, and microcook at 100% power 3 minutes. Add flour, curry powder, and cloves, and stir well. Recover and microcook at 100% power 45 seconds. Stir in stock slowly, recover, and microcook at 100% power 2 minutes. Add apple, raisins, lemon juice, zest, and reserved chicken. Stir well. Recover and microcook at 100% power 3 to 4 minutes, stirring twice. Serve over hot cooked rice.

Mid-Eastern Chicken

TWO-DINNER CHICKEN

*2 servings each
for 2 meals*

salt, freshly ground
   pepper, and paprika
   to taste
1 Holly Farms Fryer, or
   Split Chicken, or Whole
   Chicken Quartered

melted butter or
   margarine for brushing
Hot Fruit Sauce or
   Horseradish and Chive
   Sauce (below)

If using a whole fryer, split chicken in half lengthwise. Season chicken on all sides with salt, pepper, and paprika. Place, skin side down, on rack in broiler pan and brush lightly with melted butter. Broil 4 inches from source of heat, 10 minutes. Turn chicken over, brush with melted butter, and broil 10 minutes. Continue broiling and turning chicken for total cooking time of 35 to 45 minutes or until chicken is cooked through. (Use tongs, rather than fork, to turn chicken.) Serve half of chicken immediately with Hot Fruit Sauce (below). Allow remaining half chicken to cool. Wrap cooled chicken and store in refrigerator or freeze for use another time. Serve cold (thaw if frozen) with Horseradish and Chive Sauce (below).

Hot Fruit Sauce:

1/2 cup peach, apricot, or
   pineapple preserves
2 tablespoons hot water

2 teaspoons lemon juice
1/4 teaspoon ground cloves

Place all ingredients in saucepan. Cook over low heat, stirring, until preserves are melted. Spoon over broiled chicken and serve.

Horseradish and Chive Sauce:

1/2 cup heavy cream
2 to 3 tablespoons
   prepared horseradish,
   drained, or freshly
   grated horseradish
2 tablespoons snipped
   chives

1 teaspoon sugar
1/2 teaspoon Dijon-style
   mustard
   salt and white pepper
   to taste

Beat cream just until thickened. Add horseradish, chives, sugar, mustard, salt, and pepper, and stir well. Cover and refrigerate. Serve chilled sauce with either hot or cold chicken.

Variation: Add 1/4 cup peeled, seeded, finely diced cucumber.

Microwave Method:　Season chicken with salt, pepper, and paprika. Add 1 teaspoon browning sauce to melted butter. Brush chicken and place, skin side down, in single layer in shallow microproof baking dish, placing thickest part of chicken at outer edge of dish. Cover and microcook at 100% power 10 minutes. Turn chicken over, brush with melted butter and browning sauce, recover, and microcook at 100% power 8 to 10 minutes or until chicken is tender. Let stand 5 minutes. Serve hot or cold as directed above.

To Microwave Fruit Sauce:　Place preserves, hot water, lemon juice, and cloves in 1-cup glass measure and stir well. Cover loosely and microcook at 100% power 1 to 2 minutes or until preserves are just melted. Spoon over chicken.

CUMIN CHICKEN　　　　　*2 servings*

2 tablespoons vegetable oil	2 teaspoons creamy peanut butter
4 Holly Farms Prime Chicken Thighs or 2 Prime Chicken Thighs and 2 Prime Chicken Drumsticks	3/4 cup homemade chicken stock (page 24) or canned chicken broth
1 onion, thinly sliced	1/2 teaspoon cumin seed, crushed or 1/2 teaspoon ground cumin
1 tablespoon all-purpose flour	salt and freshly ground pepper to taste

Heat oil in skillet. Add chicken and brown on both sides. Remove chicken with tongs and place in shallow glass baking dish. Preheat oven to 350°F. Add onion to skillet and sauté until transparent. Add flour and peanut butter and cook, stirring, 1 minute. Gradually stir in stock and cook until mixture is thickened and comes to a boil. Remove sauce from heat, stir in cumin, salt, and pepper. Pour sauce over chicken. Cover and bake 50 minutes or until chicken is tender. Serve hot.

Microwave Method:　Brown chicken and prepare sauce as directed above. Arrange chicken in 1 1/2-quart microproof baking dish, placing thickest part of chicken pieces towards outer edge of dish. Pour sauce over, cover loosely, and microcook at 100% power 8 minutes. Turn chicken over, baste with sauce, recover, and microcook at 100% power 6 to 7 minutes or until chicken is cooked through.

CLASSIC CHICKEN à la KING   *12 to 14 servings*

1/2 cup plus 2 tablespoons
    butter or margarine
1 pound mushrooms, thinly
    sliced
1 green pepper, seeded
    and chopped
1/2 cup plus 2 tablespoons
    all-purpose flour
4 cups light cream or
    half and half
2 cups homemade chicken
    stock (page 24) or
    canned chicken broth
1/3 cup dry sherry

1/2 teaspoon dry mustard
    salt and white pepper
    to taste
    dash cayenne
5 cups cubed cooked
    chicken (page 93)
1 cup canned or frozen
    tiny peas, cooked and
    drained
1 jar (4 ounces) sliced
    pimientos, drained
1/3 cup toasted slivered or
    sliced almonds for
    garnish

Melt butter in large deep saucepan. Add mushrooms and green pepper and sauté about 5 minutes or until green pepper is just about tender. Stir in flour and cook 2 minutes over low heat. Add cream and stock slowly and cook over low heat, stirring, until sauce is thickened and comes to a boil. Reduce heat, stir in sherry, mustard, salt, white pepper, and cayenne. Add chicken, peas, and pimientos. Stir gently and simmer just until heated through. Spoon mixture into large chafing dish and sprinkle almonds on top. Serve over hot cooked rice or noodles, toast points, English muffin halves, or in baked patty shells.

Cookin' With
Holly Farms

Chicken — there is a difference!

There is a good reason why "America is Cookin' With Holly Farms." Not too long ago, chicken was just chicken. The consumer had no way of knowing where it came from or how long it had been in the store. You just had to trust your butcher, if you knew your butcher.

Holly Farms changed all that. It has revolutionized the industry by researching, experimenting, and developing advanced techniques in production, processing, and packaging. These techniques are your guarantee that you will get a product that is not only superior in taste, texture, and freshness — but also one that is competitively priced. As a result, Holly Farms has become the nation's largest marketer of fresh chicken and our products are available in many major supermarket chains.

We are proud and pleased that our customers have increased by more than 50 percent over the past five years, and that the number of satisfied Holly Farms customers continues to grow. In fact, our research tells us that customers will even drive miles out of their way to buy a Holly chicken!

Holly Farms, based in Wilkesboro, North Carolina, maintains a total of 8 processing plants in several states to insure quick delivery and fresh, high-quality chickens. The company employs 10,000 people and maintains its own fleet of 1,700 vehicles.

HOLLY-PAK® — packaging made perfect:

The Holly-Pak method of packaging chicken — pioneered by Holly Farms in 1964 — is the main reason why Holly Farms can

THE HOLLY-PAK® LABEL

This label is your guarantee of Holly Farms® Quality Assurance.

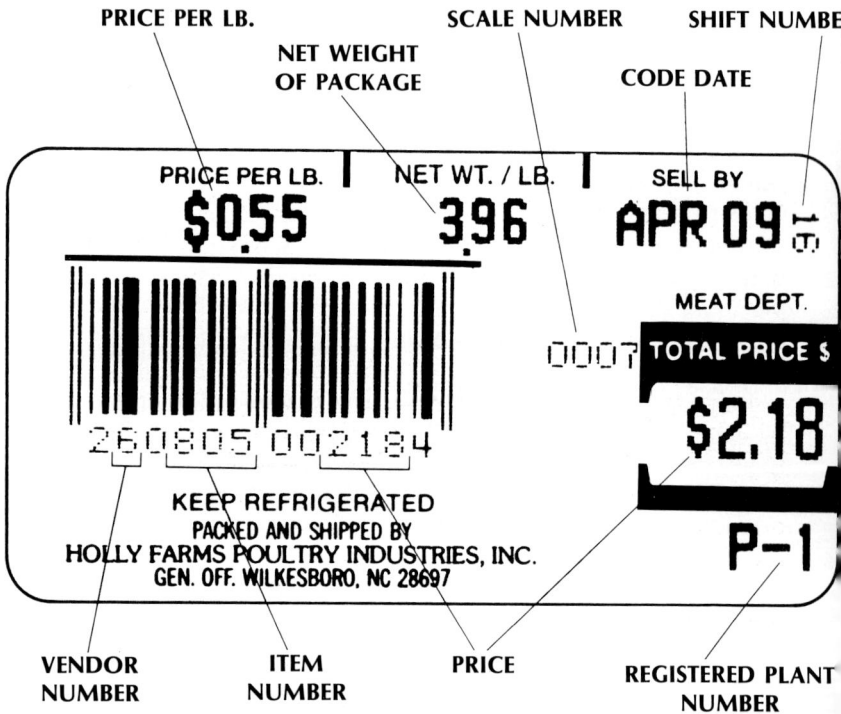

The Holly-Pak label illustrated above is a complete buying guide for you. It includes many features that help you, your grocer, and Holly Farms make certain that our products reach you at their prime. The large, prominent display of our open code dating is one of the most important features of our Quality Assurance policy.

offer you a product of exceptional taste, freshness, and cleanliness. It takes the guesswork out of buying chicken.

Ordinary chickens arrive at your supermarket either ice-packed or frozen. (The freezing method is usually restricted to whole birds.) When chickens are packed in ice, they absorb a significant amount of moisture, causing a water weight gain and decreased flavor. The chicken goes through numerous temperature changes being loaded, transported, temporarily stored, then cut and repackaged. The butcher at each retail outlet must cut chickens with his own equipment and package them for his own display case. This extra handling can increase spoilage and shorten shelf life. In fact, the average ice-packed or frozen product will maintain freshness only about one-half the time of a Holly Farms chicken.

In contrast, the Holly Farms chicken arrives at the store sealed in its own protective Holly-Pak, as fresh as when it left Holly Farms. At our modern processing plants, chicken is quickly chilled to a temperature of 28° to 32° Fahrenheit. While you may see some ice crystals on the surface of the chicken, this temperature does not freeze the chicken, and the meat is still pliable if you squeeze it. This process retains the original flavor, insures freshness and nutrient content, and helps to retard bacterial growth.

In the Holly-Pak process, chicken is cut, packaged, and sealed by Holly Farms so it is never handled from the time it leaves our spotless U.S.D.A.-inspected plant until you open it at home. No more exposure to icy water, backroom cutting and packing operations, or uncontrolled shipping methods that might increase the amount and rate of bacterial growth.

Holly-Pak offers freshness up to seven days — unheard of in the ice-packed product. And the method uses a minimum of water, so there is no leakage, no mess. In addition, our chickens are knife-cut, rather than saw-cut, so there are no bone splinters.

Open-code dating is yet another advantage of the Holly-Pak packaging method. This label is put on Holly Farms chickens in our plant at the time of packaging. The date on the label shows the last day the product should be displayed, even though it will still be fresh for four days after that if it is stored properly. If frozen, it will last even longer. All other information is right there on the package: types and number of pieces; total weight; price per pound; total price; and selling expiration date (See opposite). Our name and address are right there on the package, so that you know whom to contact. Holly Farms is responsible for all the chicken it sells and affirms that with its guarantee on every package.

Total product control for freshness and safety:

The Holly-Pak packaging and distribution method is the final stage of a total, disciplined program of quality assurance which starts with the egg and goes all the way to the homemaker's table.

Our staff and field service force constantly monitor our hatcheries, breeder farms, and broiler farms. We use only the finest feed formulas, and ingredients are carefully checked and analyzed for quality and insurance against contamination. Holly Farms complete, modern processing plants assure you of clean, fresh chicken, every time.

A cooperative program with the United States Department of Agriculture helps to assure freshness, safety, and high quality of products. All Holly chickens are U.S.D.A. inspected and Grade A. Even before each chicken is graded, it is inspected by the U.S.D.A. for wholesomeness and given the inspection seal carried on the package. This is your assurance of a healthy, wholesome product.

The highest grade that can be given to chicken by the U. S. Department of Agriculture is Grade A. This grade is based upon meatiness and appearance of every individual chicken or piece. Nationally only one chicken in three carries the Grade A shield. Every Holly Farms whole chicken and packaged chicken has the Grade A shield!

To make sure Holly Farms chicken is delivered to the marketplace fast, we have our own fleet of refrigerated trucks. So our product gets to your supermarket quickly, under carefully controlled temperature conditions, and with Holly Farms personnel watching all the way.

Nutritious is also delicious and economical:

Chicken is a meat that is good, and good for you. So Holly Farms has developed a variety of products to let you include this high-protein, low-fat meat frequently in your menu.

Holly Farms chicken provides you with a variety of cuts to satisfy your recipe and family needs without any waste. There are more than 40 different items and package sizes, so you can buy just what you need and want.

Holly Farms Chicken Franks let you enjoy that traditional favorite, the hot dog, with 25 percent less fat, 14 percent fewer calories, and 20 percent more protein, but with the same great taste as found in traditional meat hot dogs. Our taste tests with thousands of consumers have proven that our chicken franks are as great tasting as the best beef franks! Holly Farms also produces Chicken Franks with Cheese, Chicken Bologna, Chopped Chicken with Barbeque Sauce, and Chicken Ring Sausage in both mild and hot varieties.

INDEX

153

Index